FOOD

25 AMAZING PROJECTS

INVESTIGATE THE HISTORY AND SCIENCE OF WHAT WE EAT

Kathleen M. Reilly

Illustrated by Farah Rizvi

green press INITIATIVE

Nomad Press is committed to preserving ancient forests and natural resources. We elected to print *Food: 25 Amazing Projects Investigate the History and Science of What We Eat* on 4,007 lbs. of Williamsburg Recycled 30% offset.

Nomad Press made this paper choice because our printer, Sheridan Books, is a member of Green Press Initiative, a nonprofit program dedicated to supporting authors, publishers, and suppliers in their efforts to reduce their use of fiber obtained from endangered forests. For more information, visit www.greenpressinitiative.org

Nomad Press
A division of Nomad Communications
10 9 8 7 6 5 4 3 2 1
Copyright © 2010 by Nomad Press
All rights reserved.

This book was manufactured by Sheridan Books,
Ann Arbor, MI USA.
July 2010, Job # 318368
ISBN: 978-1-934670-59-0

Illustrations by Farah Rizvi

Questions regarding the ordering of this book should be addressed to
Independent Publishers Group
814 N. Franklin St.
Chicago, IL 60610
www.ipgbook.com

Nomad Press
2456 Christian St.
White River Junction, VT 05001
www.nomadpress.net

Contents

Other titles in the *Build It Yourself* series

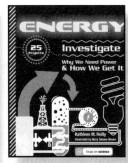

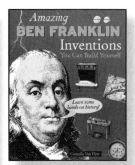

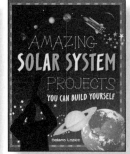

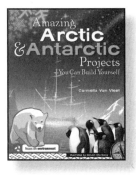

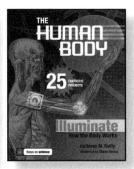

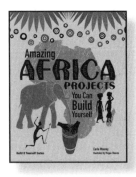

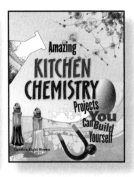

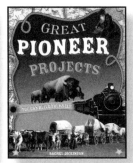

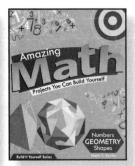

Feeling Hungry?

When you are hungry for a snack, you can just grab something out of the freezer and pop it in the microwave. It is hot and ready in seconds to eat in front of your high-def television.

If your parents wanted a snack at your age, they might have grabbed a box of sugar cereal and poured themselves a bowl to eat while they watched Saturday morning cartoons. And if your grandparents had wanted a snack at your age, they might have pulled an apple off the backyard tree before catching a show on the radio.

What about your ancient **ancestors**? Maybe they plucked some berries off a bush, or had to wait for their next meal instead. (And they didn't even have electricity, so forget about TV or radio!)

1

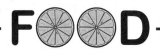

F☉☉D

FOOD HAS CHANGED OVER THE YEARS, AND SO HAS THE WAY WE THINK ABOUT IT, GET IT, AND EVEN GROW IT.

FOOD FOR THOUGHT

Food is important in a lot of different ways. It gives us the energy we need to live. It plays a central role in many of our holidays and celebrations. And it helps connect us to our ancestors.

Favorite family recipes are passed from generation to generation, and we all have special memories that involve food. Do you remember a delicious pie that your grandmother baked for you, or the first time you climbed an apple or orange tree and picked ripe fruit? Or maybe you've used gourds to decorate the Thanksgiving table.

Some of the foods we eat have changed over time, while others have stayed the same for thousands of years. New recipes have been created, and old ones re-discovered. Food is **nutrition** for your body. But it can also be something poetic and beautiful. The bottom line is that food is a big part of our lives. It's part science, part history, and part **culture**.

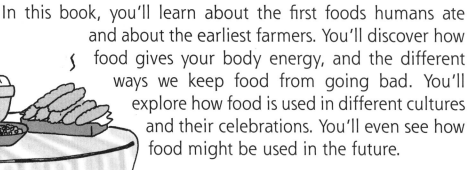

In this book, you'll learn about the first foods humans ate and about the earliest farmers. You'll discover how food gives your body energy, and the different ways we keep food from going bad. You'll explore how food is used in different cultures and their celebrations. You'll even see how food might be used in the future.

Ready to follow food across space, time, and history? Grab a snack, and let's go!

WORDS to KNOW

ancestor: people from your family or country that lived before you.

nutrition: the vitamins, minerals, and other things in food that your body uses to stay healthy and grow.

culture: the beliefs and customs of a group of people.

2

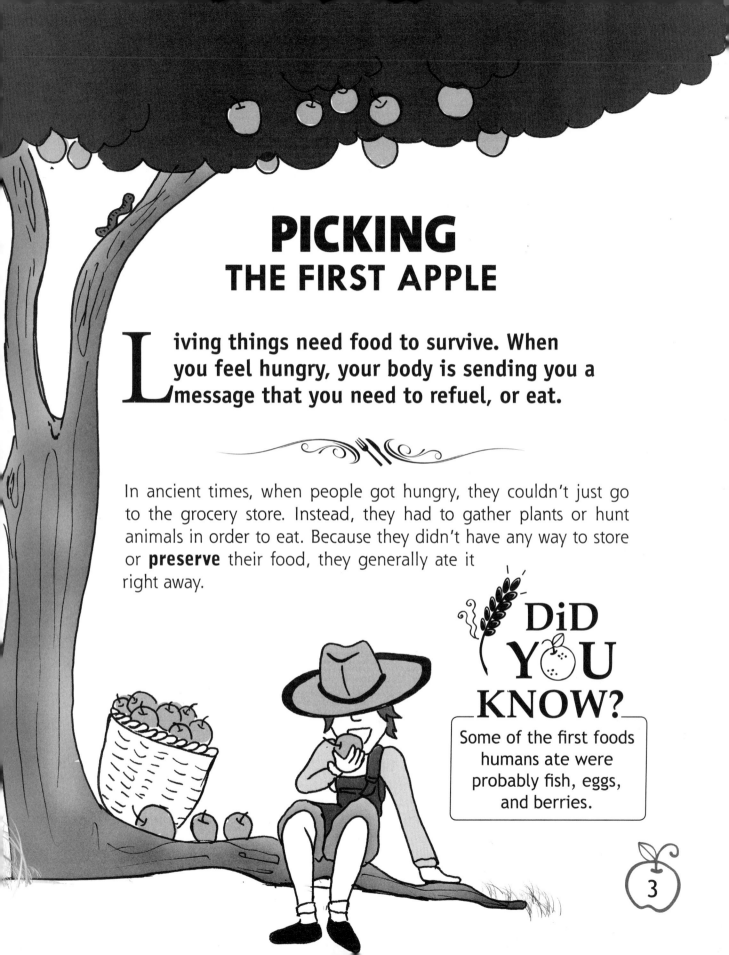

PICKING
THE FIRST APPLE

Living things need food to survive. When you feel hungry, your body is sending you a message that you need to refuel, or eat.

In ancient times, when people got hungry, they couldn't just go to the grocery store. Instead, they had to gather plants or hunt animals in order to eat. Because they didn't have any way to store or **preserve** their food, they generally ate it right away.

DiD YOU KNOW?

Some of the first foods humans ate were probably fish, eggs, and berries.

3

Ancient people were **nomads** who moved around to find food. They followed herds of **migrating** animals and looked for places where plants were ripening. There was no guarantee that they would always find food when they needed it, and people often went hungry.

Eventually, people realized they could plant seeds and grow **edible** crops themselves. They could settle in one place and create a steady supply of food for themselves.

Ancient Egyptians learned to grow crops along the **Nile River**. During the first part of the farming season, the Nile would **flood**, depositing **fertile** soil on the fields along its banks. While the fields were flooded, people fished for food. When the waters receded, the people planted seeds in the rich soil left by the flood.

MAKING IT LAST

When ancient people began farming, they were still limited by the seasons and the weather. After all, they couldn't grow crops during cold winters, or during floods or **droughts**. So they needed to figure out ways to save their food for times when it wasn't as plentiful. Unlike us, they couldn't just put their leftovers in the refrigerator or the freezer.

WORDS to KNOW

preserve: to save food in a way that it won't spoil, so it can be eaten later.

nomads: people who move from place to place in search of food.

migrate: to travel to the same place at the same time each year.

edible: safe to eat.

Nile River: a long river in Africa (4,132 miles or 6,650 kilometers) that winds its way from Burundi to Egypt.

flood: when a dry area is covered by water.

fertile: land that's able to produce vegetation.

drought: a period of very dry weather when there is not enough rain.

dehydrate: to remove the moisture from something.

microorganism: anything living that is so small you can only see it with a microscope.

fermentation: a chemical reaction that breaks down food.

ANCIENT PEOPLE DEVELOPED SEVERAL METHODS TO PRESERVE THEIR FOOD.

One of the simplest techniques to preserve food was to dry it in the sun, **dehydrating** it. Drying food removes the moisture that allows **microorganisms** to grow. Microorganisms spoil the food. Another way to dry food was to slowly smoke it over the fire.

Native Americans made a food called pemmican by grinding together dried meat and fruit with fat. They carried pemmican on long trips, and also ate it during the winter, along with dried corn and beans.

Another technique for preserving food was called **fermentation**. This is a natural process that occurs when food starts to break down, or decay. This produces acids that stop or limit the growth of the microorganisms that cause food to spoil. Ancient people developed a way to control the process of fermentation using yeast.

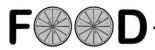

Yogurt is a food produced through fermentation. Ancient people may have made the first yogurt as far back as 4,500 years ago. Because milk is so **perishable**, early people may have turned most of it into yogurt and cheese, which are foods that keep longer.

Another important form of food preservation is **salting**. Salt also limits the growth of the microorganisms that spoil food. For many ancient cultures, fish was a major source of food. To make fish last longer, it was often salted.

People also used spices to preserve their food. And some pickled their food, which involved immersing it in vinegar to slow the growth of microorganisms. Meanwhile, fruit could be preserved by soaking it in honey, and meat preserved by sealing it with fat to keep out the air.

HOW OLD IS THAT FOOD YOU'RE EATING?

Many of the foods that we eat and drink today first originated in ancient civilizations. The steaming mug of hot chocolate that you enjoy when it's cold outside, for example, has a very long history, dating back to the ancient Maya.

WORDS to KNOW

perishable: easily spoiled.

salting: using salt to preserve food.

The Maya lived in Central America and are believed to have created a chocolate drink about 2,000 years ago. They served it cold. First they ground cocoa seeds into a paste. Then they mixed this paste with ingredients like water, chili peppers, and cornmeal. This made a bitter, frothy drink, not much like the sweet, creamy treat that you drink today.

The drink was adapted by the Aztecs, another ancient group of people. The Aztecs sometimes added vanilla, but it was still very bitter and spicy.

After Spanish explorers invaded Central America and conquered the Aztecs, they brought the drink back to Europe. Over time, the spices were removed and sugar added to sweeten it. In the late 1600s, the water was replaced with milk to make the drink creamier.

The marshmallow is another food that originated a long time ago. The ancient Egyptians made the first marshmallows about 4,000 years ago. They extracted a sweet substance from the marsh mallow plant, a wild herb that grew in marshes. Then they mixed the substance with honey to sweeten and thicken it. This produced a candy that was only offered to rulers and gods.

DiD YOU KNOW?

The first popcorn dates back about 5,500 years. The Aztecs used it in their dance ceremonies in the 1500s!

Around 1850, marshmallows underwent a significant transformation. French candy makers mixed the mallow root sap with egg whites, corn syrup, and water. They heated the mixture up and poured it into molds, making marshmallows similar to the ones we eat today. Today, machines create the white puffs that we know so well.

MAKE YOUR OWN
ANCIENT HOT CHOCOLATE

The hot chocolate that you drink today is very different from the concoction sipped by ancient people. To see how it all started, give this recipe a try.

Make sure you have permission from an adult to use the stove.

Supplies

- 8 ounces bittersweet or Mexican chocolate
- 2 small saucepans
- spoon and whisk
- stove
- up to 2 teaspoons chili powder, depending on your taste
- 5 cups milk (or light cream, if you prefer a thicker drink)

- 2 cups water
- 1 vanilla bean, split lengthwise, or 1 teaspoon vanilla extract
- 1–2 cinnamon sticks, or ½–1 teaspoon ground cinnamon
- up to 2 tablespoons sugar or honey, depending on how sweet you want it
- whipped cream (optional)

1 Break the chocolate into small pieces and set aside. In a small saucepan, heat the water to boiling. Whisk the chili powder into the boiling water and set aside to cool.

2 In the other small saucepan, slowly heat the milk, stirring often. Add the vanilla and cinnamon.

3 Remove the saucepan containing the milk from the stove and stir in the chocolate and sugar. Whisk well, and return the saucepan to the stove, dropping the temperature down to low heat.

4 Stir the mixture until the chocolate is melted and all the ingredients are thoroughly combined.

5 If you used a vanilla bean and/or cinnamon stick, remove them now.

6 Slowly add the chili water to the milk mixture. Test as you go to make sure the chili is not too overpowering.

7 If your hot chocolate is too thick for your taste, add more milk to thin it.

8 Pour your hot chocolate into mugs and top with whipped cream.

MAKE YOUR OWN
MARSHMALLOWS

Ancient people used a plant to make marshmallows, but that's not how we make them today. If you've never created your own marshmallows before you're in for a treat! They're easy to make, and they taste fantastic! Make sure you have adult supervision.

1 Pour the gelatin and ½ cup of the cold water into the mixer bowl. Let stand.

2 Heat the other ½ cup of water in the saucepan until it is boiling. Stir in the sugar, corn syrup, and salt, and then cook the mixture over medium high heat, covered, for approximately 4 minutes.

3 Test the temperature of the sugar mixture with the candy thermometer. Continue to cook the mixture until it reaches 240 degrees Fahrenheit (115 degrees Celsius). This should take about 8 minutes. As soon as the mixture reaches the right temperature, remove it from the heat.

4 Start the mixer at slow speed, and carefully pour the sugar mixture down the side of the bowl. When all of the sugar mixture has been added to the gelatin and water mixture, turn the mixer up to high speed. Add the vanilla. Whip the mixture until it is thick, about 14 minutes.

5 While the mixture is thickening, stir together the powdered sugar and cornstarch. Dust the bottom and sides of the pan with this powder.

6 Pour the thickened mixture into the pan, making sure it is evenly spread. Dust the top of the mixture with the sugar-cornstarch powder.

7 Let the marshmallows sit uncovered for 4 hours. Then flip them out onto the cutting board, using the pizza cutter to slice them into squares.

8 Dust all sides of the marshmallows with the sugar-cornstarch powder to keep them from sticking together. Enjoy!

Supplies

- 3 packages unflavored gelatin
- 1 cup of ice cold water, divided
- stand mixer
- stove
- saucepan with cover
- 1½ cups sugar
- 1 cup light corn syrup
- ¼ teaspoon salt
- candy thermometer
- 1 teaspoon vanilla
- ¼ cup powdered sugar
- ¼ cup cornstarch
- 9-by-13-inch pan
- cutting board
- pizza cutter

MAKE YOUR OWN
DEHYDRATED FOOD

Modern methods of preservation, including refrigeration, allow food to last a long time today. But if you're camping or hiking, you need food that won't spoil. Try this recipe for homemade jerky, which is dried beef. Make sure your family doesn't need the oven for a while—it takes about 6 hours to dry the beef! You'll need an adult to help cut the meat.

1 Put the beef in the freezer for about an hour. This will make it firmer and easier to cut.

2 Ask an adult to cut the beef against the grain into slices about an eighth of an inch thick. Set these slices aside.

3 Open one of the zipper bags and prop it up inside a bowl so it will stay open as you add ingredients.

4 Add the spices and sauces to the bag. Seal the bag and squish all the ingredients around until they're well blended.

Supplies

- refrigerator/freezer
- 1 pound lean beef
- cutting board and knife
- 2 gallon-sized zipper bags
- bowl
- ½ cup soy sauce
- ½ cup Worcestershire sauce
- 1 tablespoon brown sugar
- 1 teaspoon garlic powder
- 1 teaspoon onion powder
- 2 teaspoons liquid smoke
- oven
- baking sheet with sides
- aluminum foil
- cookie rack
- airtight container

5 Add the beef, and reseal the bag. Squish everything around again until the beef is completely coated with the sauce/spice mixture. Refrigerate the bag of beef strips overnight.

6 The next day, preheat your oven to 160 degrees Fahrenheit (70 degrees Celsius), and then cover the baking sheet with aluminum foil to protect against drips. Place the cookie rack on top of the aluminum foil on the baking sheet. This will allow the strips of beef to drip their juice onto the sheet below.

7 Remove the bag of beef strips from the refrigerator, and lay them across the cookie rack on the baking sheet in a single layer.

8 Put the meat in the oven. Depending on how thick the slices are, it will take 4 to 6 hours (or even more) to dry into jerky.

9 The jerky is ready when it's completely dry and chewy. You can test the readiness of the jerky by putting a cooled slice into the other zipper bag and sealing it. If the bag fogs up (this is called condensation), the jerky is not ready yet. However, be sure the beef has completely cooled before you put it in the bag, or you'll get condensation from the temperature change. If you dry the beef too long, it will become brittle and crumbly.

10 Store your jerky in the airtight container.

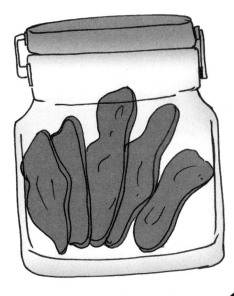

MAKE YOUR OWN
FLOODING NILE

The ancient Egyptians relied on the flooding cycle of the Nile River to give them fertile soil for their crops. In this activity, you'll create your own miniature Nile to produce a tiny "crop" of grass.

1 Fill the cookie sheet with a layer of soil. Use the knife to make trenches in your soil matching the general outline of the Nile River. Be sure to include the part where the river forks, forming the delta. This is the triangle of land at the mouth of the river where it meets the sea.

2 Use sheets of plastic wrap to line the trenches. This will keep most of the water inside your "river" and prevent it from just soaking into the soil.

3 Place pebbles in the trenches to keep the plastic wrap down. Plant grass seed along the "river" banks.

4 Carefully pour some water into your "river." Let it fill up and slowly overflow its banks, watering the grass seed.

5 As the soil dries out, flood your "river" every few days. Soon, you'll have grass growing.

Supplies

- small cookie sheet with edges
- potting soil
- knife
- map of the Nile River
- plastic wrap
- small pebbles
- grass seed
- water

FARMING, PAST & PRESENT

I t's almost dinnertime! You put down your book and head to the kitchen to get the chicken out of the refrigerator for your mom. There it is, neatly wrapped in plastic wrap on a foam tray. Your brother elbows past you to grab the green beans out of the freezer. They're already washed and cut, just waiting to be tossed into the microwave or steamer. As your brother sets the table, your dad pours glasses of cold **pasteurized** milk from a plastic jug.

You know that the food you're about to eat didn't just come like that. In order to reach you, that food travels a long way, and undergoes a series of changes. This whole process starts with the farmer.

15

Farming, or **agriculture**, is one of the oldest jobs in history. At first, people only grew enough crops to provide for their own needs. As time went on, however, farmers produced enough food to support others, who were then able to take on other jobs.

WORDS to KNOW

pasteurized: food that has been heated to destroy harmful bacteria.

agriculture: production of food through farming.

climate: average weather patterns in an area over a period of many years.

livestock: animals on a farm that produce food like milk and eggs, or products like wool.

produce: fruits and vegetables.

In many parts of the world today, a relatively small group of farmers produce enough food for everyone else. Agriculture has become a huge business in modern countries like the United States. Food is produced in one location and shipped far away to many others. Frequently, you don't even know how, or where, the food you're eating was produced.

THE FIRST SEED

The agricultural process takes a lot of work. Farmers can't just drop any seeds they want into the ground and, months later, return to collect their harvest. Many factors determine what can and can't grow.

One of these factors is the location of the farm. Different crops grow in different **climates** and soils. This is why you won't find pineapples growing in New York, or cucumbers growing in the tropical rainforest. Some plants thrive in dry heat, while others need cooler temperatures and moisture. Farmers are limited to what they can grow in their area.

FARMERS MUST ALSO ADJUST TO THE WEATHER. TOO MUCH RAIN AND PLANTS MAY ROT IN THE GROUND. OR A LATE FREEZE MIGHT KILL THEM. WEATHER CAN RUIN A CROP.

THE MEAT YOU EAT

Crops aren't the only thing farmers raise. They also keep **livestock**. These are animals such as sheep, cows, and pigs that are used to produce food such as milk and meat, or other important products, such as wool. Animals on the farm can also serve as a source of labor, by pulling plows or carrying heavy loads. On larger farms, however, most animals have been replaced by machines.

Some farms specialize in less traditional livestock. They raise creatures like ostriches, llamas, or buffalo. Today, more consumers are interested in new meats that may be healthier alternatives to beef.

FROM THERE TO HERE

Imagine that you're walking in a peach orchard. You're hungry, and pick a peach to eat. Which peach would you rather have: one that's soft and juicy, or one that's hard as a rock?

DiD YOU KNOW?

A hard-boiled ostrich egg takes 40 minutes to cook! One ostrich egg is equal to two dozen chicken eggs.

Grocery stores know that most people prefer soft and juicy. That's why they try to stock their bins with **produce** that's either at its peak of ripeness or just about to reach it. However, think about that trip from farm to market. As quick as businesses try to make it, there's still going to be some delay. This means that many crops are picked before they're actually ripe, so that they are just ripening as they reach stores.

Back in the late 1930s, the first "farm to market" road was finished in Texas to bring crops from the farm to the market as fast as possible. These "FM" (for "farm to market") roads connected rural areas to more populated ones. Today, most produce is shipped by land, air, and sea to its markets.

HOW DO FRUITS AND VEGETABLES RIPEN?

Most fruits and vegetables that are ready to ripen produce **ethylene gas**. The gas triggers **enzymes** to start the ripening process—usually making the fruit or vegetable less green, softer, and often sweeter. The riper it gets, the more gas it produces. If the fruit or vegetable keeps ripening and making ethylene, it will eventually start to rot.

Keeping fruits and vegetables cool in your refrigerator will slow down ripening. Since refrigeration doesn't completely stop ethylene production, you still need to eat produce before it goes bad.

Fruits that ripen after picking...

Apricots	Kiwi
Avocado	Peaches
Bananas	Pears
Cantaloupe	Plums

...and fruits that don't

Apples	Oranges
Cherries	Pineapple
Grapefruit	Strawberries
Grapes	Watermelon

SUPER-SIZED FARMING

For centuries, farming employed more people than any other industry. But in the late 1700s, machines began to change things. Farms didn't need people as much because machines could work faster than humans or animals.

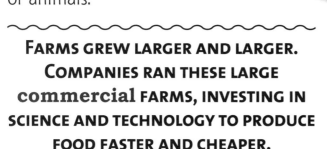

FARMS GREW LARGER AND LARGER. COMPANIES RAN THESE LARGE commercial FARMS, INVESTING IN SCIENCE AND TECHNOLOGY TO PRODUCE FOOD FASTER AND CHEAPER.

Some people resist this type of farming, calling it "mega-farming." They say that it harms the land by stripping it of its natural nutrients. The **pesticides** and **herbicides** used to protect the crops can damage the **environment** and pose health risks to people who eat this food.

Some people also argue that "mega-farming" has negatively affected the variety of crops grown today. For example, it's easier to mass-produce a single type of tomato than many types, because each may have different needs.

WORDS to KNOW

ethylene gas: a natural ripening agent produced by many fruits and vegetables.

enzyme: a natural chemical that causes a reaction.

commercial: large businesses producing large quantities.

pesticides: chemicals used to kill or control insects.

herbicides: chemicals used to kill unwanted plants like weeds.

environment: a natural area with plants and animals.

 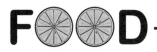

WORDS to KNOW

genetic engineering: manipulating genes to alter appearance and other characteristics.

heirloom plants: plants that were grown earlier in human history.

ROBOTIC PRODUCE

Consumers tend to want produce that looks perfect. Today's produce also has to survive the long journey from farm to market.

With farmers trying to make the most profit by producing super-resilient and attractive foods, many have turned to **genetic engineering**. This involves manipulating plants to produce crops with the qualities farmers and consumers want. Hardier plants can also decrease the amount of herbicides and pesticides that need to be used.

But there's a flip side. Genetically enhanced plants or animals can interfere with natural processes. They can outcompete natural species and disrupt ecosystems. They can acquire weaknesses as well as strengths, and even pose a risk to the humans that eat them.

Partially in response to the use of genetic engineering, many small farmers are growing **heirloom plants**. These are descendants of plants that a group of people has passed down over many years. They reproduce naturally and are spread through hand cuttings.

FARMERS WHO GROW HEIRLOOM PLANTS MAY WANT TO KEEP THESE PARTS OF HISTORY ALIVE, OR PRODUCE SOMETHING THEY KNOW HASN'T BEEN SCIENTIFICALLY CHANGED.

MAKE YOUR OWN
HARVEST EXPERIMENT

In this activity you can see how the ethylene produced by fruit speeds ripening.

Supplies

- 1 bunch of bananas
- 2 pieces of unripe produce such as peaches
- paper bags

1 Place a banana and a piece of unripened fruit out in the open air. Do not place them near each other. This will be your "control" fruit, the pieces that you aren't doing anything to, and thus your basis for comparison.

2 Place one banana in a paper bag by itself. Place one banana in a paper bag with one of the pieces of unripe produce.

3 Leave all of the fruit for 2-3 days, and then check them out. Which banana ripened fastest? Which peach ripened fastest? Did the banana have a significant impact on the ripening of the other produce?

4 Don't eat anything that's rotted. Put it out in the compost bin instead.

BRR...IT'S CHILLY IN HERE!

With the invention of the refrigerated railroad car and the development of commercial canning, farmers were able to ship their produce farther than their local marketplace. Large-scale commercial farming grew quickly, especially in states with long growing seasons like California.

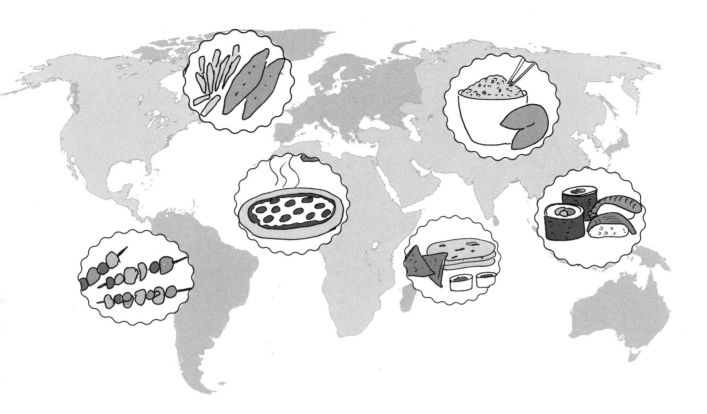

FOOD & CULTURES

Imagine if scientists wanted to put things into a space capsule to share information about Earth with any aliens that might encounter it. Your job is to find foods that represent different parts of Earth. (Fortunately, the capsule has a special seal that prevents food from spoiling, so the aliens won't end up with a tube of fuzzy green mold!)

Some parts of the planet are easy to represent. For example, rice for Asia. Other parts of the world, however, might be tougher, like Australia. Why is this? Why do some areas have traditional foods?

Most likely, it's because some cultures have developed around specific foods. Rice has been central to Asian culture for about 10,000 years. It's so important that, in many Asian languages, the words for rice and food are identical. Rice is also a common theme in Asian art.

Rice needs warm weather and plenty of water to grow. In some areas, the fields of rice are actually flooded with water. These fields are called rice paddies. Farmers often work knee- or thigh-deep in water as they tend their crops in the paddies.

> **ACROSS ASIA, PEOPLE DEPEND ON RICE AS A FOOD SOURCE AND AS A SOURCE OF INCOME.**

SICK TATERS

It is easy to choose a food to represent Ireland. The potato comes from South America, where it was first grown by the ancient Incas. In the early 1500s, European explorers looking for gold discovered the potato, and brought it back across the Atlantic.

Very quickly, the potato became essential to the diets of the people of Ireland. It was filling, cheap, and easy to prepare. Potatoes were especially important to the poor.

The problem is that potatoes were at risk from diseases in the new land that were not found in South America. When diseases hit the potato crops in the 1700s and early 1800s, there were many years that the potato crop failed. The farmers and the economy managed to recover from these failures.

DiD YOU KNOW?

On average, a person in Asia eats about 300 pounds of rice every year. The average American eats about 25 pounds of rice every year.

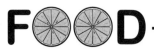
Between 1845 and 1852, the potato crop was attacked by a devastating disease called the **potato blight**. It destroyed the potato crop to the point that many people starved and the economy collapsed. This period is known as "The Great Famine."

DiD Y⦿U KNOW?

The potato is grown in more places than any other food crop.

By the end of the **famine**, almost a million people had died of starvation. Another million had fled Ireland, seeking food and jobs in North America and Australia. During the Great Famine, the population of Ireland dropped from about nine million to just over four million people.

IT'S A-MAIZE-ING

If you're looking for a food from Africa to put into the space capsule, you might try cornmeal. Also called maize, cornmeal is made from ground dried corn. Maize is central to people's diets in many African countries. It is often served as porridge, with vegetables like yams, cabbage, or turnips added to it for flavor. In countries like Zimbabwe, people either buy pre-ground cornmeal or grind their own from their crops.

Cornmeal is called different things in different African communities:

Zimbabwe: *sadza*
Kenya: *ugali*
Uganda: *posho*
Malawi: *nsima*
South Africa: *mealie pap*

MELTING POT

Now think about your own family. Do you have a staple food item, something that forms the base for just about every meal you eat? Probably not. Like most Americans, you eat a variety of foods. You might dine on fried rice and sweet-and-sour chicken one night, and then have pizza and salad or barbecued chicken and mashed potatoes another night.

24

There are a few reasons for this. Since the United States covers a wide range of climates, farmers can grow different things. We have a reliable transportation network capable of bringing these foods across the country.

In addition, people from all over the world have settled in the United States. They've brought many different types of foods with them. If you like to eat a variety of foods, you're fortunate to live here!

WHAT'S IN YOUR SHOPPING CART?

What your family eats can be influenced by your heritage, your financial status, and where you live. If you live in the country, you may have fewer choices than if you live in a big city.

National and world events affect what you eat too. **Immigrants** settling in different areas of America during the early 1900s opened a variety of restaurants. That's why there are so many Italian pizzerias in New York City and Creole establishments in New Orleans.

During World War II, **rationing** influenced eating patterns. Meat, sugar, and butter was available only in limited quantities to the general population. Why? These foods needed to be sent to soldiers fighting the war.

WORDS to KNOW

potato blight: a disease that destroys potato crops.

famine: a period of great hunger and lack of food for a large population of people.

immigrant: someone settling in a new country.

rationing: when the supply of something is limited and it is distributed carefully among people.

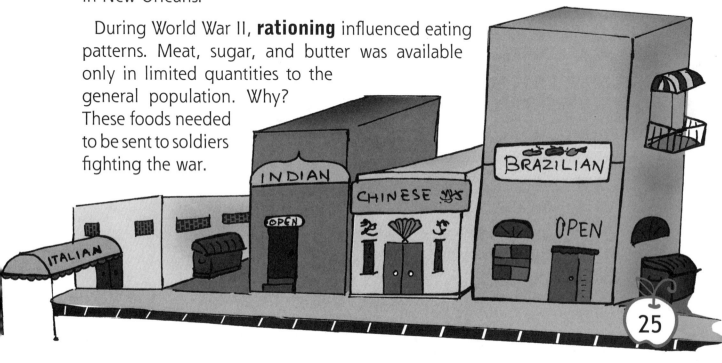

MAKE YOUR OWN
POTATO MAZE

The lowly potato has fed millions of people and become an important part of many cultures' diets. Make this maze to help a potato find its way . . .

1 Cut two pieces of cardboard that will fit very snugly as dividers inside the shoebox.

2 Using the scissors, cut a small hole, about half an inch wide, in a different place on each divider. These holes will be the way your potato works its way through the "maze."

3 Using the duct tape, secure the dividers into the shoebox, spacing them evenly. Your shoebox should now have three sections. The potato's sprouts will work its way through the holes, so make sure there aren't any other openings in your shoebox.

Supplies

- shoebox with a lid
- cardboard
- scissors
- duct tape
- potato that's beginning to sprout

4 Cut a large hole about 1 inch wide in the end of the shoebox. Make sure the lid won't cover it up. This is where the sunlight will expose the potato.

5 Place your potato in the first compartment of the shoebox, the one farthest from the sunlight hole.

6 Put the lid on the shoebox. Tape it securely if you need to. Place the shoebox where the sunlight will shine on it.

7 Keep checking your box. After several days, the potato should have found its way through the maze and out the hole at the end of the box! Take off the lid, and you can see how it navigated its way. The sprout was growing toward the light, like all plants do.

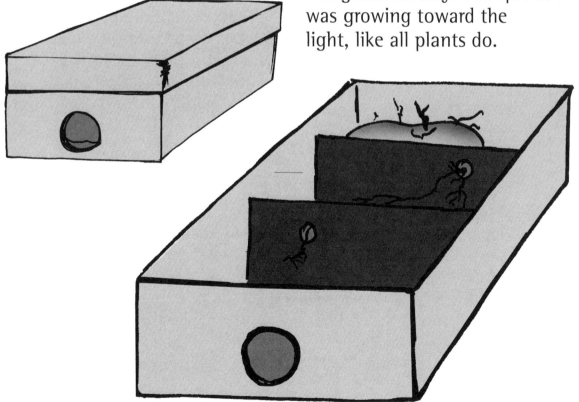

MAKE YOUR OWN
RATION CAKE

During World War II, bakers got creative to meet the challenges of rationing. They came up with ways to make things like eggless cakes and meatless meals. This recipe was a base for whatever else was on hand, like fruit, pudding, or ice cream.

1 Preheat the oven to 350 degrees Fahrenheit (175 degrees Celsius).

2 In a small saucepan, mix together the water, raisins, cinnamon, cloves, nutmeg, sugar, shortening, and salt.

3 Bring this mixture to a boil and boil for 3 minutes. Remove it from the heat and allow it to cool.

4 In a large bowl, stir together the flour, baking soda, and baking powder, and then stir in the mixture from the saucepan. Pour the combined mixture into the pan.

5 Bake for about 50 minutes, checking for doneness every so often.

Supplies

- oven
- mixing spoons
- small saucepan
- 1 cup water
- 1 cup raisins
- 1 teaspoon cinnamon
- ¼ teaspoon cloves
- ½ teaspoon nutmeg
- 1 cup brown sugar
- ⅓ cup shortening
- ¼ teaspoon salt
- large bowl
- 2 cups flour
- 1 teaspoon baking soda
- ½ teaspoon baking powder
- loaf pan or 8-inch square pan

MAKE YOUR OWN
GALI AKPONO

Gali Akpono is an African cornmeal cookie flavored with nutmeg.

1 Preheat the oven to 350 degrees Fahrenheit (175 degrees Celsius).

2 In a small bowl, mix the cornmeal with the water. In a large bowl, mix together the flour, sugar, salt, and nutmeg.

3 Add the cornmeal mixture to the flour mixture and stir together. Mash the margarine into the flour-cornmeal mixture with a pastry cutter or fork.

4 In the small bowl, whisk together the eggs and the milk. Save the white from one of the eggs for later. Add the milk and eggs to the flour/cornmeal mixture.

5 Roll the dough out about quarter inch thick. Use a biscuit cutter or the top of a glass to cut the dough into small circles, about 3 inches across. Brush the top of each cookie with egg white.

6 Bake the cookies on a cookie sheet for about 12 minutes, until they are golden-brown.

Supplies

- oven
- mixing spoons
- mixing bowl
- 1 cup cornmeal (white or yellow)
- 2 tablespoons water

- 1½ cups flour
- ¾ cup sugar
- ¼ teaspoon salt
- ½ teaspoon nutmeg
- ½ cup margarine
- pastry cutter or fork

- 2 eggs (1 egg separated)
- 1 cup milk
- rolling pin
- biscuit cutter
- pastry brush
- cookie sheet

I WANT IT!
FOOD IN DEMAND

Food has a way of traveling around the world. People try something new and find it so delicious that they just have to share it with family and friends. Or someone realizes that a certain food from one place can be sold profitably in another. In ancient times, some foods were so valuable that they were used as money.

Spices like cinnamon, ginger, and turmeric were highly prized in ancient Asia and the Middle East. As European explorers traveled eastward, they encountered these spices and wanted them, too.

Spices were so expensive that only the very wealthy could afford them. Outlandish stories were told to explain the high cost of spices. The ancient Greek writer Herodotus claimed that people who gathered cinnamon had to fight against "winged creatures like bats which screech horribly and are very fierce." Another Greek philosopher said that deadly snakes guarded cinnamon. These tales were untrue, of course, but they made spices seem even more exotic and valuable.

WORDS to KNOW

palatable: when something tastes okay.

embalm: to preserve a body.

People used spices to improve the taste of food, or even to make it **palatable** to begin with. They also used spices to make perfume, preserve meat, create medicines, and even **embalm** the dead.

With European demand for spices high, traders in Asia, the Middle East, and Egypt became very wealthy. They kept the origins of their spices a secret, so no one could compete with them and ruin their profits.

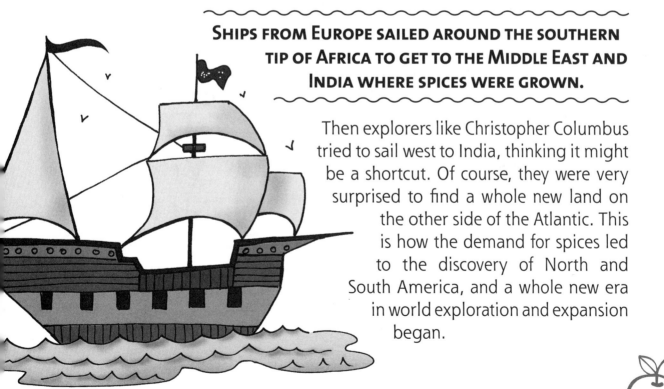

SHIPS FROM EUROPE SAILED AROUND THE SOUTHERN TIP OF AFRICA TO GET TO THE MIDDLE EAST AND INDIA WHERE SPICES WERE GROWN.

Then explorers like Christopher Columbus tried to sail west to India, thinking it might be a shortcut. Of course, they were very surprised to find a whole new land on the other side of the Atlantic. This is how the demand for spices led to the discovery of North and South America, and a whole new era in world exploration and expansion began.

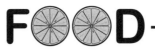
CARE FOR A CUP?

The ancient Chinese began drinking tea 5,000 years ago. It was often used for medicinal purposes. As Chinese explorers and conquerors traveled across Asia, the Middle East, and eventually Europe, they brought tea with them.

BIGGEST NUT YOU'VE EVER "SEED"!

Coconut has also traveled around the world, but a little differently than spices or tea. Experts don't agree on exactly where the coconut palm tree originated. Some think it came from South Asia, while others believe it's South America. Today, coconut palms grow throughout the tropics.

Coconuts spread partly through human activity, when ancient travelers carried them with them. But they also spread naturally. Because coconuts float, they were carried by ocean currents around the world, even as far north as Norway!

WHAT'S INTERESTING ABOUT THE COCONUT IS THAT IT'S NOT ACTUALLY A NUT, BUT RATHER ONE GIANT SEED FROM THE COCONUT PALM!

DiD YOU KNOW?

The coconut got its name from the word "cocho," which means ghost or boogeyman, because of its weird "face."

HOW MUCH IS THAT BANANA IN THE WINDOW?

If you're vacationing near the beach, chances are you'll want a good seafood dinner. And it will probably taste far better than anything you get back home. Why is that?

It's because the fish is fresher. Food produced or grown locally is not only fresher—it's usually cheaper too. Seafood, for example, is generally more expensive the farther you get from the coast. That's because you're paying to have the fish shipped to you.

Some foods can also cost more out in the country. This is not only because of transportation costs, but because there are fewer people to buy food there. Lower demand causes supermarkets to increase prices to make money.

That's why it's a great idea to shop and eat locally. Not only will you get fresher food, but it will probably cost less, too. For the same reason, you should eat what's in season. When you eat something that's out of season, there's a strong chance that it grew in another climate, like South America. It had to get shipped quite far to reach you.

What's in season?

January: broccoli, citrus fruits like oranges, grapefruits, lemons

February: citrus fruits, papayas, cauliflower

March: pineapples

April: asparagus, spring peas

May: cherries, apricots

June: blueberries, melons, strawberries

July: corn, summer squash, green beans, peaches, raspberries

August: peaches, plums, melons, tomatoes, summer squash

September: pumpkins, grapes, pomegranates

October: sweet potatoes, apples, winter squash

November: bananas, greens, winter squash

December: sweet potatoes, papayas

MAKE YOUR OWN
PRICE SHEET

Even at stores within your own neighborhood, prices for groceries can vary, sometimes by as much as a dollar or more per item. With a price sheet you'll be able to compare and tell when you've found a good deal—or when you've come across a rip-off. Help your family stay on top of the lowest prices with this price sheet.

Supplies

- blank paper
- calculator
- grocery receipts from recent trips to the store
- grocery store ads

1 Draw a chart. Label the first column "Food" and the other columns "Unit Price for _____," putting in the names of the grocery stores where your family shops. You should have one column for each store your family uses.

2 Under the "Food" column, write down a list of food products that your family normally buys. List general products like milk, eggs, bread, chicken, lettuce, etc. You should also list specific products, like cereal brands, because the price varies depending on what kind you buy. Don't worry if you can't think of everything. This is just the beginning of your price sheet.

3 Find the total price for each product at the stores that you have listed. You can look at recent grocery receipts and ask your parents.

4 Now figure out the unit price of each product at each store. Look at the unit of measurement for each product. Take the price paid for that product and divide it by the number of units in the package.

For example, if there are 16 ounces of orange juice in a carton and it costs $1.50, take $1.50 and divide it by 16. The answer ($0.09) is your unit price, or how much the juice costs per ounce. If you bought this juice at Foodie Mart, you would put the unit price of $0.09 per ounce under the "Foodie Mart" column in the "juice" row.

UNIT PRICE

Unit price describes how much the item costs per pound, ounce, or whatever unit of measure is used. It allows you to easily compare items, such as an 8-ounce box of crackers for $1.75 (with a unit price per ounce of $0.22) with a 13-ounce box of crackers for $2.49 (with a unit price per ounce of $0.19, which is a better deal). At the store you can find the unit price for items right on the shelf.

5 Now look at grocery store ads. Figure out the unit prices for the products on sale to see if the sales really are a good deal.

6 Use your price list to help your family shop. You can stock up during great sales and shop at stores that give you the best values. Add to your price list as often as you can. With more prices you'll be able to make wise shopping decisions.

MAKE YOUR OWN
SPICE MIX

In the past, spices were extremely valuable. Although we don't pay as much for spices today, some pre-made spice combinations can be expensive. If you mix your own blends you can save money, as well as have fun.

You can make your own mix by smelling or tasting a little bit of each spice and combining them according to what you think will be good. Or, try some of these combinations. Put the spice mixes in an empty salt or pepper shaker and just shake out how much you need onto your food.

CAJUN SPICE MIX

- 1 teaspoon white pepper
- 1 teaspoon black pepper
- 1 teaspoon ground red pepper
- 1 teaspoon garlic powder
- 1 teaspoon onion powder
- 1 teaspoon paprika

APPLE PIE SPICE MIX

- 1 teaspoon ground allspice
- 1 teaspoon ground cardamom
- 2 teaspoons ground nutmeg
- 4 teaspoons ground cinnamon

TACO SPICE MIX

- ¼ teaspoon garlic powder
- ¼ teaspoon onion powder
- ¼ teaspoon dried oregano
- ¼ teaspoon crushed red pepper flakes
- 1 tablespoon chili powder
- ½ teaspoon paprika
- 1½ teaspoons ground cumin
- 1 teaspoon sea salt
- 1 teaspoon black pepper

FOOD PACKAGING

When people began growing crops, they stored food by wrapping it with natural materials such as shells, gourds, animal skins, reeds, bark, and leaves. Eventually, people wove grasses and reeds into baskets. For thousands of years, this was all the packaging humans needed.

About 8,000 years ago, ancient people in the Middle East realized that they could benefit from storing their food in more **durable**, heavier containers. The first pots were simple balls of clay with holes carved into them, or long coils of clay molded into a round shape.

WITH THE INVENTION OF THE POTTERY WHEEL, PEOPLE BEGAN MAKING MORE COMPLEX POTS.

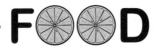

Glazing the pottery made it more durable. The glaze also kept water from seeping into the clay. Potters took pride in the pots they created, and had their own "mark" or pattern that they'd use to identify which pots were made by them.

"WOOD" YOU HOLD THIS?

Ancient Egyptians started using wood to make boxes for storing food. Wooden boxes were lighter, less fragile, and less cumbersome to move than pots. Two thousand years ago, people in Syria figured out how to blow glass and make the first glass containers.

Metal containers came next. Although silver and gold were used for cups, these were too valuable to use for food packaging. Tin was used instead. Later, inexpensive containers made from thin aluminum were used to package all kinds of food.

ALTHOUGH PLASTIC WAS INVENTED IN THE MID-1800S, PLASTIC FOOD PACKAGING ARRIVED MUCH LATER.

The next major **innovation** in food packaging was plastic. Plastic wrap, plastic containers, and Styrofoam all changed the way food was packaged and how long it lasted. Without proper packaging and storage, food will spoil and go to waste.

Advances in Packaging

1310: First paper packaging in England.

1817: First cardboard boxes for packaging in England, 200 years after the Chinese invented cardboard.

1830: First metal boxes for packaging. Cookies, and then cakes, were sold in these.

1844: Rise of paper bags for packaging.

1900: Rise of glass bottles for packaging liquids.

1950: First aluminum foil containers for packaging. The first "TV dinners" were packaged on aluminum trays.

1950: Rise of aluminum cans for packaging.

1958: First plastic "shrink wrap" used for packaging.

CAN THIS THING OPEN?

The metal food containers of the 1800s weren't like the ones on your shelf today. Manufacturers sealed cans in a completely different way.

Cans were **soldered** together by hand. A small hole was left open on the top of the can. Food was crammed into this hole, which was then covered with a patch. But one tiny hole was left open. This hole let out steam while the food cooked right in the can. After cooking, the hole was sealed so no air could get into the can.

WORDS to KNOW

durable: able to last.

innovation: new idea or invention.

solder: to fuse metal together to form one piece.

complex carbohydrate: a food source such as whole grains or beans that gives you energy.

DiD YOU KNOW?

Until 1866, the only way to open a sealed can of food was to use a hammer and chisel!

Then   Now

This canning method was so time-consuming that only about 60 cans could be made and filled in a day. After 1866, consumers used a "key" to roll a metal strip away from the side or top of the can, exposing the food inside. The can opener was invented in 1875, making this entire process a lot easier.

PICKING THE PERFECT PRODUCT

Let's say you've got a big soccer game coming up, and your coach has told you to eat a breakfast high in **complex carbohydrates** to give you enough energy for the game. You go to the store to shop for breakfast and turn down the cereal aisle.

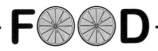

WORDS to KNOW

biodegradable: something that living organisms can break down.

organism: anything living.

bioplastics: plastic made from plant material.

non-renewable: energy sources that can be used up, that we can't make more of, such as oil.

sustainable: a resource that cannot be used up, such as solar energy.

A bright yellow box catches your eye. Mmmm . . . Fruity Bombs! You love the taste of fruit, you think the character on the box is cool, and there's a sweet prize inside! You grab the Fruity Bombs and head home.

But if you'd read the nutrition information on the side of the box, you'd realize there are zero complex carbohydrates in this sugar-filled bonanza in a box.

What just happened? You got caught up in the advertising. Manufacturers want packaging to do more than just hold their products. They want boxes that convince you to buy their product over everyone else's.

PACKAGING SELLS THE PRODUCT.

Would you rather buy a plain brown box of spaghetti or a box with a photo of an amazing spaghetti meal, complete with steaming meatballs and freshly baked

bread, on the front? When you're in the store, remember that companies are trying to sell you their product. They spend a lot of money designing packaging to get your attention.

It's important to know what you really need and want when you head to the store. If you buy the plain brown box of pasta, you could end up saving money—maybe enough to buy bread to go with your meal!

HUG THE PLANET!

Paper and cardboard dominated the packaging industry for most of the last century. By the late 1970s, plastic became more popular.

Not using paper saves a lot of trees. But plastic doesn't break down as easily as paper. This garbage has become a major problem for our environment.

Experts are coming up with new ways to reduce the environmental impact of packaging. They've developed **biodegradable** plastics with the starch from plants like corn, wheat, and potatoes. These **bioplastics** break down much more easily than traditional plastics. While traditional plastics are made from **non-renewable** oil resources, these bioplastics are made from renewable resources, so they're much better for the planet.

Have you ever opened a box of cereal or crackers and found the plastic bag inside only half full? Companies designed this packaging hoping to give the impression there was more food.

DiD YOU KNOW?

A bottle can take around 1,000 years to break down. A paper bag takes just a couple of months.

NOW MANY COMPANIES ARE TRYING TO BE MORE sustainable AND USE LESS PACKAGING.

You and your family can help the environment by making smarter food choices. Eat more fruits and vegetables that require no packaging (other than Mother Nature's!) and food that has minimal packaging. You'll probably be eating healthier, too!

MAKE YOUR OWN
CLAY POT

In this activity, you'll make a coil pot similar to the ones that our ancestors made to store their food. Don't put any food in your pot, however, unless it's in another wrapper. The clay you get at stores isn't "food quality."

1 Begin by softening the clay. The heat of your hands will warm and soften the clay. Gently play with it, roll it around, and squish it. Roll a medium piece of clay into a ball and then press it flat until you get a circle about 3 inches in diameter. This will be the base of your pot.

2 Roll a large piece of clay into a long "snake." The snake should be about a half inch in diameter.

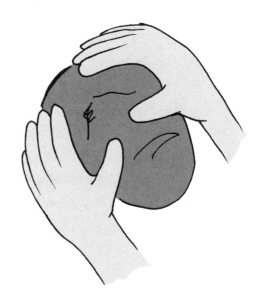

Supplies

- clay that can be air-dried or baked dry
- spray bottle filled with water
- paints (optional)

3 To build the sides of the pot, lay the end of the snake around the outside of the circle, coiling it up on top of itself to make a series of stacked rings. If you run out of snake before your pot is tall enough, just make another snake, attach it to the end where you stopped, and continue.

4 When your pot is the size you want, spray a little water on your coils and smooth them together to make the sides of your pot solid. Make sure to press the sides of your pot firmly into the base.

5 If you want to make a lid for your pot, roll another medium piece of clay into a ball and press it flat until it is the size of the top of your pot.

6 Dry your lid separately from your pot so they don't stick together. Air-dry or bake your pot. When your pot is dry, you can decorate it with paint.

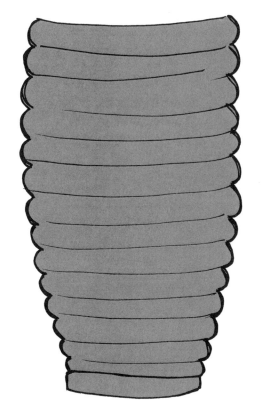

MAKE YOUR OWN
PROTECTIVE FOOD PACKAGING

Manufacturers try to come up with packaging that will protect the food inside as it's being shipped to stores. In this egg drop experiment, you'll find out just how difficult it can be to keep food safe in transit!

1 In this project, your goal is to create packaging that will protect an egg from a fall.

2 Think about the everyday materials that you have around the house. What might provide good protection for the egg? For example, you might consider cotton wool or leftover bubble wrap, or some kind of inner suspension in a plastic container.

3 Create several types of packaging for a few different eggs. That way, you can test to see which is most effective.

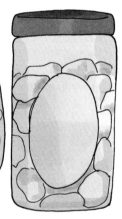

4 When your eggs are safe in their packaging, either drop them from a high place or throw them as high as you can—and get out of the way!

Supplies

- raw eggs
- supplies for packaging (see step 2 for ideas)

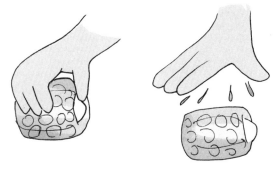

ASK YOURSELF:

a. Why are things like crackers in a plastic bag inside a cardboard box?

b. Why isn't milk in a see-through plastic jug, like soda?

c. How do manufacturers protect food like potato chips?

5 Carefully open up all the packages. Think about why some eggs survived and others didn't. Then consider the packaging that real manufacturers use.

Some food, like the crackers, needs protection from moisture that makes it go stale quickly. Other food, like the milk, loses vitamins when exposed to light for too long. And some food, like the potato chips, crushes easily and needs to be cushioned with air or a rigid tube. When you buy certain foods, you're also paying for their special packaging!

MAKE YOUR OWN
CATCHY PACKAGE

Packaging not only has to protect food, but it also has to attract the consumer—you!—and make you want to buy the product. In this project, you'll try to come up with your own eye-catching package.

1 Take your notepad to the grocery store. Walk up and down the aisles and look at the ways that companies present their products. How do they use color? Slogans? Characters? Who is the audience? Are they appealing to moms, kids, or both? Take notes on what you observe.

2 Then come home and look through your pantry. Pick a "boring" item that you're going to market—plain saltine crackers, maybe, or spaghetti.

3 Think about how best to convince someone that he or she absolutely must have *this product*. How can you make it stand out from other products on the shelves? What are its major benefits? Convenience? Great taste? Versatility? Also, keep in mind the audience to whom you are trying to sell this product.

Supplies

- notepad
- pencil
- food you're going to "sell" (see step 2 for ideas)
- 3 plain cardboard boxes, such as shoeboxes
- markers, stickers, paint, or other things to decorate with

DiD YOU KNOW?

In commercials, only the food being advertised has to be real. The food around it can be fake to make it look good. The ice cream being sold might be real, but that whipped cream could be shaving cream!

4 Develop three different package designs. Apply each package design to a different box.

5 Show your packages to your parents, brothers, sisters, and friends, and ask them which one they'd be most likely to choose. Tally the results. The more input you get, the better.

6 When you've received all your feedback, go through the results. Every time companies develop a new product or redesign an old product, they go through this same process. Keep this in mind the next time that you go grocery shopping. When you buy a product, are you making your decision based on the packaging or the food inside? Could the generic store brand, with the same taste at a lower price in less attractive packaging, be a better choice?

FOOD SAFETY

When you eat something, you assume you're not going to get sick from it. That's because today's governments work hard to ensure that our food is as safe as it possibly can be.

It wasn't always that way. After the **Industrial Revolution** in the late 1700s and early 1800s, food began to be transported farther distances. The distance between where food was produced and where it was consumed grew.

At the same time, food became more and more processed. Companies developed new products like canned pie filling, canned soup, and canned chili. Machines did more of the work, replacing people who could watch every step. With increased processing came a greater chance that something bad could happen to the food.

BEFORE FOOD MANUFACTURERS WERE regulated BY THE GOVERNMENT THEY COULD ADD THINGS TO THE FOOD THEY MADE—OR JUST IGNORE WHAT ACCIDENTALLY ENDED UP IN THERE!

WORDS to KNOW

Industrial Revolution: the name of the period of time that started in the late 1700s in England when machines replaced people as a way of manufacturing.

regulated: controlled by rules or laws.

IT'S A JUNGLE OUT THERE

During the early 1900s, an author named Upton Sinclair spent a lot of time in Chicago researching his new novel, *The Jungle*. Sinclair's goal was to write about the plight of American workers, many of whom worked for extremely low pay under terrible circumstances. In *The Jungle*, he specifically discussed the horrifying conditions in meat-packing plants.

When he published the book in 1906, readers were appalled more by its descriptions of the unsavory aspects of meat processing than by the poverty of the workers. They demanded change—and they got it. The Meat Inspection Act and the Pure Food and Drug Act of 1906 required food processing plants to undergo regular inspections and maintain high standards. The Act showed that food safety was now a public concern.

DiD YOU KNOW?

Despite our best efforts to keep food safe, an estimated 76 million cases of food-borne illness (or food poisoning) occur each year in the United States.

About 20 years later, the U.S. government created the Food and Drug Administration (FDA) to enforce the rules established by the Pure Food and Drug Act. Today, the FDA monitors the safety of food, medicines, vaccines, cosmetics, pet food, and many other products.

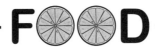

SIDE ORDER OF GERMS?

Food is much safer now than in Upton Sinclair's day. But you still have to make sure to properly handle and cook your family's food to avoid food poisoning by **bacteria**.

In most cases, these bacteria won't kill you. However, being sick definitely isn't fun, so be sure to take extra precautions with uncooked meat in your kitchen. When you dine out, eat hamburger that is completely cooked and has no pink inside at all.

Common forms of food poisoning caused by bacteria.

SALMONELLA is a bacteria that lives in the intestines of animals. If you eat something contaminated by salmonella you can suffer diarrhea, fever, and abdominal cramps for up to a week. Protect yourself by not eating raw or undercooked eggs and meat, and by keeping raw meat away from other foods in your refrigerator. Use separate cutting boards to cut raw meat and other foods. Also, wash your hands immediately after touching birds or reptiles, which can be carriers of the bacteria.

E. COLI is a bacteria that lives in the intestines of cattle. When you cook ground beef, cook it long enough to raise the temperature inside high enough to kill any bacteria that might be lurking there. Ideally, your hamburger should not be pink inside.

CAMPYLOBACTER is a bacteria that lives in the intestines of birds. Avoid eating undercooked chicken. Also, don't store raw chicken in your refrigerator so any juice can drip down onto other food.

WORDS to KNOW

bacteria: microorganisms found in soil, water, plants, and animals that are sometimes harmful.

expiration date: the date food should be eaten by.

WHEN FOOD TURNS UGLY . . .

While proper handling and packaging can postpone the decay or spoilage of food, eventually the food will go bad. That's why manufacturers put an **expiration date** on packages. This tells consumers when the food should be used.

If you look at expiration dates on different products, however, one may say "use by," while another may say "expires on." Turns out, they all mean slightly different things.

Unfortunately, the labeling of foods is an inexact science, because it's hard to predict exactly when packaged foods will spoil.

AS THE SAYING GOES, "WHEN IN DOUBT, THROW IT OUT."

It's a good idea to eat any fresh meat within two days of bringing it home from the store. Why? Because in the store, the meat is kept at a chilly 30 degrees Fahrenheit (-1 degree Celsius). Inside your home refrigerator, it's usually warmer than that. Bacteria can start to grow on meat when temperatures rise, especially if the meat has a lot of surface area, like ground beef. You can also freeze meat for up to three months.

IF IT SAYS . . . IT MEANS

Sell by . . . After this date, grocers should take the product off the shelves. Depending on what the product is, they may discount it and sell it for a short time at a reduced price.

Use by . . . After this date, you shouldn't eat the product.

Best before . . . The quality or flavor of the product will be best if you eat it before this date.

Best if used by . . . The same as "best before."

Expires on . . . After this date, the product will be unsafe to eat.

Ancient additives included natural things like salt and vinegar, which were used to preserve food. Today, some additives are still natural, while others are artificial, or made from chemicals.

Milk is often packaged in cardboard or **opaque** plastic containers to prevent it from losing vitamins when it's exposed to light. If milk is pasteurized, it can stay fresh for about five days past its "sell by" date.

DO YOU RECALL . . .

You may have heard in the news about certain foods being **recalled**. In 2009, the FDA recalled almost 4,000 products containing peanuts because of concerns about salmonella contamination. The recall included everything from peanut butter and ice cream to pet food. Recalls show that our food safety system is working the way it should.

ADDING IT UP

Sometimes manufacturers add substances to food products. These are called **additives**, and they're used to change the food's color, appearance, taste, and **longevity**. By using additives, manufacturers hope to make their products more appealing.

Some additives may not be very healthy for you. For example, food dyes used in the past made some people sick. Although the FDA tests additives for safety, people can have allergic reactions to them.

If you're concerned about additives in the products you eat, check the ingredient list on the packaging. Look to see if something was added.

WORDS to KNOW

opaque: not clear.

recalled: when an entire batch of food is returned to the manufacturer because of a safety issue.

additive: something added to food to change its characteristics.

longevity: how long food lasts.

allergen: something that triggers an allergic reaction.

histamines: chemicals that protect the body against allergens.

IF THE LABEL SAYS . . . IT'S USED TO

Sodium nitrates . . . color, flavor, and preserve foods, as well as help prevent the growth of the bacteria that cause botulism, a form of food poisoning.

Aspartame . . . artificially sweeten foods.

BHA and BHT (butylated hydroxyanisole and hydroxytoluene) . . . preserve foods, and especially to prevent oils from going bad.

MSG (monosodium glutamate) . . . flavor foods.

Sulfites . . . preserve foods, and especially prevent discoloration in dried fruits and other products.

Artificial colors . . . change the color of food to improve its appearance.

BAD REACTIONS

Sometimes people experience an allergic reaction to certain kinds of food. They can develop a rash, have their lips or face swell up, or have a hard time breathing.

DiD YOU KNOW?

Common foods that cause allergic reactions include eggs, milk, nuts (including peanuts), wheat, shellfish, fish, and soybeans.

Food allergies occur when a person's body is sensitive to an **allergen** present in certain foods. Suppose a person is allergic to peanuts. When this person eats peanuts, his or her body responds to the peanuts as though they are invaders. The body jumps into action—overreaction, in this case—and tries to fight off the "invaders" by releasing chemicals called **histamines**. These chemicals produce the symptoms of an allergic reaction: a rash, swelling, and/or trouble breathing.

53

MAKE YOUR OWN
HOME FOOD SAFETY WATCH

Play food detective in your own house and protect your family from any unsafe foods that might be lurking. Bring the following checklist to your kitchen and cross off each item as you complete it.

1 First, check the expiration dates on the perishables in your refrigerator. If you have raw meat that was purchased more than two days ago, put it in the freezer or eat it tonight. Throw out any dairy products that are past their expiration dates, and make a note to eat or drink others that are approaching their dates.

2 Check to make sure the raw meat is stored in a bin or below the fresh foods in your refrigerator, so it can't drip any juices on them.

Supplies

- paper
- pencil or pen
- thermometer

3 Leave the thermometer in the refrigerator for about an hour, and then check the temperature. It should be between 35 and 38 degrees Fahrenheit (1–3 degrees Celsius). If your refrigerator is any warmer, your food may spoil faster.

4 Make sure that everyone who uses your kitchen washes their hands before and after handling food, especially raw meat and eggs. Cooking utensils and counter surfaces should also be thoroughly scrubbed down before and after use.

5 Designate one cutting board for raw meat, fish, and poultry and another for bread and produce.

6 Cook all meats thoroughly, especially meat with a lot of surface area, like hamburger.

7 Make sure to use up anything that's been defrosted. Never put food back in the freezer to re-freeze.

8 Copy this checklist and hang it up in your kitchen. Refer to it often to make sure your kitchen stays in top shape!

HOW RECALLS WORK

1. When people become ill after eating a product, they call the FDA to report their experience.

2. The FDA investigates, and, if necessary, works with the manufacturer to issue a recall.

3. The FDA and the manufacturer notify the public about the recall.

4. During the recall the FDA and the manufacturer work together to pinpoint exactly what the cause of the sickness is.

5. After they identify the problem, the manufacturer corrects it, and then ships out the new product.

6. The FDA helps the manufacturer make sure that the problem doesn't happen again.

MAKE YOUR OWN
FOOD ADDITIVE EXPERIMENT

In this activity, you'll see for yourself that taste is influenced by the color of food.

1 Beat egg whites with electric mixer until very stiff. Add vanilla and salt and blend together.

2 Add sugar gradually until the mixture is stiff again. Divide mixture into two separate bowls.

3 Add lemon extract and orange food coloring to one bowl. Add orange extract and yellow food coloring to the second bowl. Mix both well.

4 Drop by teaspoonfuls onto a greased cookie sheet. Bake 30 minutes at 300 degrees Fahrenheit (150 degrees Celsius).

5 Ask friends and family members to try the candy. See if they can guess the flavors correctly. Chances are, their first reaction will be to call the orange-colored candy "orange flavored" and the yellow-colored candy "lemon flavored!"

Supplies

- 2 bowls
- electric mixer
- 2 egg whites
- 1 teaspoon vanilla
- ⅛ teaspoon salt
- ½ cup sugar
- lemon extract
- orange food coloring
- orange extract
- yellow food coloring
- cookie sheet
- oven

TRADITIONS & CELEBRATIONS

Because food is so vital to our lives, it's natural for it to play a major role in our traditions and celebrations. For example, if you live in the United States, on every fourth Thursday in November you gather with your friends and family around a table loaded with all kinds of delicious foods. It's Thanksgiving, the day that Americans remember the first settlers and give thanks for the joy in their lives.

As with other traditional holidays, there are certain foods that are closely associated with Thanksgiving: turkey, stuffing, gravy, mashed potatoes, cranberry sauce, and pumpkin pie. These foods have been passed down through generations.

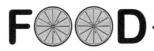

More than 45 million turkeys are eaten on Thanksgiving every year in the United States.

While some holiday customs, like those at Christmas, vary from family to family, Thanksgiving usually revolves around the same traditional menu. This menu is based on the foods that the early settlers shared with the Native Americans when they celebrated the very first Thanksgiving in 1621.

Over time, though, people have made some changes to this menu. There are some foods that we eat today at Thanksgiving that might not have been at the original feast. While there's no way to be certain exactly what was served at that first meal, historians have a good idea of what foods likely were there—and what weren't.

Traditions don't have to be complicated affairs. Have you ever gone camping and toasted marshmallows over a fire? Your parents did it when they were little, you do it now, and you'll probably do it with your own kids. It's a sweet, gooey way to share good times together.

Probably at the first Thanksgiving

Seafood like cod, eel, clams, and lobster

Wild game like turkey, goose, duck, partridge, and deer

Vegetables like beans, onions, lettuce, carrots, and peas

Fruit like pumpkins, plums, and grapes

Nuts like walnuts, acorns, and chestnuts

Possibly not at the first Thanksgiving

Ham. Although they brought pigs with them from England, the colonists probably didn't kill them to eat.

Sweet potatoes and corn. The colonists would have had dried corn, but not fresh corn because it was autumn.

Cranberry sauce. The colonists had cranberries but didn't have any sugar to make the sweet sauce.

Pumpkin pie. They probably ate stewed pumpkin instead.

Chicken & eggs. The colonists brought chickens with them from England, but may not have had any left by this time.

Milk. The colonists didn't have cows in the New World yet.

HAPPY BIRTHDAY TO YOU

Many cultures celebrate the day someone was born. For many of us, the main food event is, of course, the birthday cake. Topped with glowing candles and accompanied by the birthday song, the cake is presented to the person of honor.

> THE ANCIENT GREEKS MADE BIRTHDAY "CAKES" OUT OF HONEY OR BREAD. THEY PUT CANDLES ON TOP EITHER TO SIGNIFY THE GLOWING MOON OR TO HAVE THE SMOKE CARRY THEIR PRAYERS UP TO THE GODS ABOVE.

During the Middle Ages, people in Germany started baking cakes for "Kinderfest," celebrations honoring the birth of children. A candle in the center of each cake symbolized life. Today, we not only put candles on the cake, we also let the birthday person make a wish before blowing them out. If they blow them out in one breath, they get their wish.

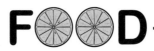
Birthday food traditions in other countries include:

- **Australia:** "fairy bread," or bread triangles with sprinkles, which are called "hundreds and thousands" Down Under.
- **China:** long noodles, to signify a long life.
- **Ghana:** a patty made from mashed sweet potatoes and eggs fried in oil, called "oto."
- **India:** a dessert called "doodh pak," which is similar to rice pudding and filled with pistachios, almonds, and raisins.
- **Mexico:** treats placed inside a piñata.
- **Russia:** a pie with birthday greetings carved into the crust.

WILL YOU MARRY ME?

Weddings are another celebration involving traditional foods. In many cultures, weddings are times to bring out special foods and drinks, things that are normally too expensive to eat.

In Mexico, for example, they serve "Mexican Wedding Cakes," which are sometimes referred to as "Mexican Wedding Cookies." These little treats are made with butter, sugar, and nuts, ingredients that were once considered "luxuries."

IN CHINA, WEDDING BANQUETS OFTEN FOLLOW A TRADITIONAL MENU. EACH FOOD THAT IS SERVED HAS A SYMBOLIC MEANING.

CHINESE DISH SERVED . . . WHAT IT REPRESENTS

Fowl, such as pigeon or quail . . . Peace

Duck or lobster . . . Happiness, since they're red, the color of happiness

Sweet red bean soup . . . 100 years of togetherness and a "sweet" life

Sea cucumber . . . Selflessness between the couple, since the word for sea cucumber sounds like the word for "good heart" in Chinese

Fish . . . Abundance, since the word for "fish" is similar to the word for "plentiful" in Chinese

7-Up . . . Happiness, since the word for "up" sounds like the word for "happiness" in Chinese

PASS THE COINS, PLEASE

The beginning of a new year fills people with hope and optimism and inspires them to make changes in their lives. People in many countries eat traditional foods on New Year's Day for good luck. In some countries, people eat 12 grapes at the beginning of the new year. They eat one grape per second, making a wish with each one. Each grape represents a month of the upcoming year, and the sweeter the grape, the better that month will be for you.

In the southern United States, black-eyed peas and collard greens are a traditional New Year's dish. The peas represent coins and the greens represent paper money. So the more of these you eat, the more money you'll make in the upcoming year!

In Denmark, people eat kale sprinkled with sugar and cinnamon because the kale looks like folded money. People in Germany, Austria, and Hungary eat pork because pigs symbolize progress. This is because pigs are always moving forward, pushing their snouts through the ground, like hard workers.

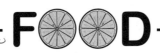
THERE ARE ALSO FOODS THAT SOME PEOPLE AVOID EATING ON NEW YEAR'S DAY. LOBSTERS ARE CONSIDERED UNLUCKY BECAUSE THEY MOVE BACKWARDS, SUGGESTING SETBACKS COULD OCCUR IF YOU ATE THEM. SOME PEOPLE ALSO AVOID ANYTHING THAT CAN FLY, BECAUSE THEY DON'T WANT THEIR GOOD LUCK TO "FLY AWAY!"

SAYING GOODBYE

In ancient times, people believed that when someone died they would need food for their trip to the next life. So large banquets were held for the person. Today, food is still served at funerals, but mainly to provide comfort to the people who are mourning their loved ones.

DiD YOU KNOW?

In ancient Egypt, people were buried with food. Egyptians thought it would feed the dead as they travelled to whatever the next world was.

In Amish communities in Pennsylvania, friends give "funeral pie" to the grieving family. They make this pie with raisins instead of fruit so it stays fresh longer, just in case the family doesn't get around to eating it for a few days.

Depending on where you live in the United States, people eat everything from casseroles to pre-made sandwiches at funerals. Meanwhile, in Belgium, people eat pistolets, which resemble hard rolls, with butter and slices of cheese.

Of course, it's not the food itself that matters as much as it is people coming together to support each other in a tough time. Food has always been an integral part of any gathering.

MAKE YOUR OWN
DOODH PAK

Traditional doodh pak is a type of sweet rice pudding, made with saffron and almonds that have been ground into a paste. This simple version will give you a sense of what it's like.

1 In a small saucepan, bring the milk to a boil. Rinse the rice with water until it runs clear, and then add it to the boiling milk.

2 Turn the heat down, and simmer the rice and milk until the rice is fully cooked. Stir frequently to prevent the rice from burning. When the rice is cooked, add the sugar.

3 Cook for another 5 minutes, and then add the raisins, cardamom, nutmeg, almonds, and pistachios.

4 Remove the doodh pak from the stove and serve hot or chilled.

Supplies

- small saucepan
- stove
- 4 cups milk
- ½ cup basmati rice
- ½ cup sugar
- ¼ cup raisins
- ½ teaspoon cardamom
- ⅛ teaspoon nutmeg
- ¼ cup almonds and pistachios

MAKE YOUR OWN
PIÑATA CAKE

In Mexico, kids celebrate their birthdays with piñatas filled with treats. While this cake isn't a real piñata, it's a cool look-alike. It takes a little effort to put together, but it's worth it.

1 Make the cake according to the directions on the box. Pour it into the small cake pan and bake. If it makes enough for two cakes, either eat one plain or make two piñatas!

2 When the cake is cool, lift it out of the pan and place it on the cutting board. The metal mixing bowl, when flipped over, needs to fit completely over your cake. If necessary, cut the cake to fit your bowl.

3 Carefully cut a shallow "scoop" out of the center of the cake. Frost the cake except for the part you scooped out. Fill that with your piñata treasures.

4 Grease the inside of the metal mixing bowl with oil, and then put it in the freezer to chill for 10 minutes. Melt three-quarters of the chocolate chips in the microwave or over a double boiler.

5 Take the metal bowl out of the freezer. Pour the melted chocolate into the bowl and carefully swirl it around so that it coats the entire inside of the bowl, including the sides. Try to coat the entire bowl with the same thickness of chocolate. Then place the bowl back in the freezer to firm the chocolate up completely.

6 When the chocolate is hard, take the bowl out of the freezer. Place the bowl upside down over the cake.

7 Using a hot, damp towel, rub the outside of the bowl to release the chocolate "shell" inside, over the cake.

8 Melt the remaining chocolate chips. Use a toothpick and the melted chocolate chips to "glue" your edible decorations to the outside of the piñata. Let the chocolate harden.

9 You're ready to party! You can use a toy hammer or the back of a serving spoon to crack open your piñata when everyone has gathered around.

Supplies

- oven
- packaged cake mix, any flavor
- eggs
- vegetable oil
- mixing bowls and spoons
- small round cake pan
- cutting board

- small metal bowl
- knife
- canned frosting
- piñata treasures like chocolate coins, rainbow chocolate chips, candies, etc.
- 16 ounces chocolate chips or melting chocolate

- freezer
- microwave
- dish towel
- edible decorations for the outside of the piñata such as chocolate nonpareils, giant sweet hard candies, gumdrops

FOOD
ACROSS TIME

We've already seen how your culture, or the environment and society in which you live, shapes what you eat. However, the *time* in which you live also affects your food choices.

Some of the foods that you eat might not have been around when your parents were kids. Let's take chicken nuggets, for example. Although chicken nuggets were invented in the 1950s, they didn't really become popular until the late 1970s, when McDonald's started serving them. Now it's hard to imagine a kid never having eaten one.

Some foods have changed over time. In an earlier chapter, you read about the way marshmallows and chocolate have been transformed over the years. Other foods, however, have endured almost unchanged. The first pretzels, for example, were created more than 1,500 years ago. They taste almost exactly the same as they did then.

Even though the United States is a young country, many styles of cooking have already come and gone. Immigrants brought foods and cooking techniques from other countries. Since they had to adapt to the ingredients available here, they had to get creative with their cooking. As a result, America has produced some unique types of food.

NATIVE AMERICANS

Long before the colonists arrived from Europe, Native Americans lived in North America. They lived in many different environments, from the dry Southwest and rainy Northwest to the forested Northeast. So they ate a wide variety of foods. The Native Americans responded to seasonal cycles and demonstrated great resourcefulness in their food choices.

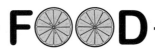

For meat, many Native American tribes relied on deer, called venison, since white-tailed deer were so plentiful. They also hunted squirrels, as well as fish and seals. On the Great Plains, tribes hunted bison for meat, too.

When fresh meat wasn't available, or when they were traveling, Native Americans depended on pemmican, which is dried meat and fruits pounded into a paste. They shaped this paste into bars, so they could easily carry it with them.

DiD YOU KNOW?

When Native Americans killed an animal for food, they thanked it for giving up its life for them.

COLONIAL AMERICA

In the 1600s, colonists from Europe settled on the East Coast of the (future) United States. The colonists quickly discovered that the soil wasn't as good as the soil in Europe. Moreover, the growing season was very short in the North. In the South, the growing season was longer, so the colonists could grow more foods. But the warm weather spoiled foods quickly.

The New World was a major challenge, food-wise, for the colonists. They didn't have food markets or shops, and some of the crops that they were used to growing didn't survive in the different climate and soil of North America. The settlers learned to use corn in foods like cornbread, hominy, and grits.

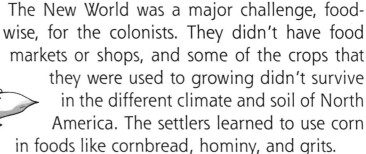

THE NATIVE AMERICANS SHOWED THE COLONISTS HOW TO GROW AND COOK NEW FOODS SUCH AS SQUASH, BEANS, PEPPERS, AND CORN.

PIONEERS AND EXPLORERS

When settlers started heading West, they had to give up a lot of their comforts. They could only bring limited supplies of food, including flour, dried beans, coffee, and sugar with them. As a result, they had to make meals without these provisions or find ways to extend what little they had.

Without access to stoves, they also had to eat foods that didn't need cooking or could be prepared easily over a campfire. To cook foods over the fire, the pioneers used cast iron Dutch ovens. These were heavy pots with lids that could also be used as skillets. The meals of the pioneers could get very creative, as they had to make do with what they had.

LUMBERJACKS

All over the United States, the population was growing quickly. As a result, the number of houses and settlements under construction skyrocketed. The need for wood created a strong demand for lumberjacks.

These groups of men moved between lumber camps, cutting down trees. They did all the work by hand, without modern equipment. Lumberjacks had to be strong and physically fit. As a result, they had to eat well.

The person responsible for feeding the lumberjacks was the camp's cook. With some assistance from his helpers, he prepared a hearty breakfast of pancakes, oatmeal bread, fried eggs, ham, bacon, and lots of coffee.

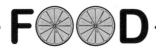
The lumberjacks usually ate lunch out in the woods. When they returned to camp, they were ravenous after a hard day's work. For dinner, the cook would supply them with large quantities of meat, beans, potatoes, and bread or biscuits. Sometimes, if the lumberjacks were lucky, the cook would make cakes or cookies to eat for dessert.

LUMBERJACK FOOD WORDS

Axle grease . . . Butter

Bait can . . . Lunch pail

Bean burner . . . Bad cook

Devil's cup . . . A tin cup without a handle, that become scalding hot when filled with fresh coffee

Fly bread . . . Raisin bread

Mud . . . Coffee

Tar . . . Really bad coffee

DiD YOU KNOW?

Pioneers on the Oregon Trail paid about 17 cents a pound for coffee. Today's coffee is around 6 dollars a pound—or more!

COWBOYS

Like lumberjacks, cowboys had hard, physically demanding jobs. They drove large herds of cattle from the ranches in Texas to markets that might be as far north as Montana and North Dakota. After rounding up the cattle, they'd begin the long journey.

Of course there weren't any drive-through restaurants on the trail, so a cook rode along with them. The cook was second in command only to the boss. All the cowboys treated the cook with respect, so he'd feed them well in return.

The cook's kitchen, called the chuck wagon, contained all the food and cooking equipment. It was filled with flour, sugar, beans, coffee, canned goods, and dried fruit. With those limited supplies, the cook had to pull together meals for all the hungry cowboys.

The prized possession of any cowboy cook was his Dutch oven, the same pot used by the pioneers. With it, the cook could make cornmeal mush, biscuits, refried beans (something Mexican cooks introduced to Texan cowboys), chili, and cobblers. This is a dessert that has fruit on the bottom and a crumbly or pastry topping.

CIVIL WAR

Lumberjacks and cowboys lived a rough life, but it was nothing compared to what soldiers in the Civil War experienced in the 1860s. Soldiers could only carry small amounts of food, and the military often had difficulty getting supplies to them.

The soldiers sometimes received salted or smoked meat and dried or canned fruits and vegetables. However, their daily allowance of food, called rations, wasn't cooked. The soldiers had to figure out a way to cook it themselves. For the most part, they survived on meat, coffee, sugar, and a dried biscuit called hardtack.

COWBOY FOOD WORDS

Airtights . . . Canned goods, like tomatoes or peaches

Prairie strawberries . . . Beans

Hot rocks . . . Biscuits

Gargle or java . . . Coffee

Hen fruit . . . Eggs

Texas butter . . . Gravy

Lick . . . Molasses

Skunk eggs . . . Onions

CIVIL WAR FOOD WORDS

Salt horse . . . Salted meat

Grab a root . . . Eat a meal, a potato

Long sweetening . . . Molasses

Goobers . . . Peanuts

Sheet iron crackers . . . Hardtack

DiD YOU KNOW?

The cowboy's cook had to get up several hours before everyone else to make meals— so he worked longer hours with less sleep out on the trail.

71

MAKE YOUR OWN
CIVIL WAR HARDTACK

This tough biscuit was carried by soldiers in the Civil War.

1 Preheat the oven to 400 degrees Fahrenheit (205 degrees Celsius).

2 In a large bowl, mix together the flour, water, shortening, and salt to form a stiff batter.

3 Spread the batter out onto a cookie sheet into a rough square that is about a half inch thick. Bake for 30 minutes.

Supplies

- oven
- large bowl and spoon
- 2 cups flour
- ½ to ¾ cup water (start with ½ cup and add in more if the batter doesn't feel moist enough)
- 1 tablespoon shortening
- salt
- cookie sheet
- knife and fork

5 Flip the hardtack over and return it to the oven for another 30 minutes. Then turn the oven off. Leave the door closed, and let the hardtack cool in the oven.

4 Remove the cookie sheet from the oven. Cut the hardtack into 3-inch squares and poke rows of holes evenly over the dough with a fork.

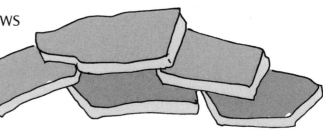

MAKE YOUR OWN
PEMMICAN

Pemmican was a portable food for many Native Americans.

1 In the food processor or blender, pulse the beef jerky until it's chopped very finely.

2 Add the dried apple slices and raisins or other dried fruit. Blend the mixture until it is thoroughly combined.

3 Dump the mixture out onto a sheet of waxed paper, and lay another piece of waxed paper on top.

Supplies

- ¼ cup dried beef jerky
- food processor or blender
- 4 dried apple slices
- ⅛ cup raisins or other dried fruit
- waxed paper
- rolling pin
- cookie sheet (optional)
- oven (optional)

4 With the rolling pin, roll out the pemmican until it's about an eighth of an inch thick.

5 Let the pemmican dry. You can leave it out in the sun for one or two days, keeping it pressed between the waxed paper the entire time. Or you can place it on a cookie sheet, removing all the waxed paper, and bake it in an oven at 350 degrees Fahrenheit (175 degrees Celsius) for approximately 2 hours. Either way, make sure to turn the pemmican over every now and then as it dries.

6 When it's completely dry, you can either cut the pemmican or just break it into pieces. Store it in the refrigerator in a sealed bag or container.

NUTRITION

When the battery in your MP3 player runs low, you plug it in to recharge. When the car runs out of gas, your parents take it to the gas station for a refill. What gives YOU energy and "power?" Food, of course!

Your body needs food to move, grow, recover from injuries, and even to think. Every time you eat something, your body tries to pull energy from it. Your job is to make sure that you eat things your body can actually use. Just as you wouldn't pour milk into your car's gas tank, you can't expect your body to run very well if you're putting junk into it.

So where does the energy in food come from? Straight from the energy cycle! Energy can't be destroyed—it just changes forms, like when a windmill converts wind energy to mechanical energy to turn the mill. Plants absorb energy from the sun and use it to grow. When animals eat the plants, the energy is transferred to them so they can use it to move and grow. When you eat plants or animals, that energy is now transferred to you—and you can move and grow!

What's In It For You?

What exactly is in food that fuels your daily activities? **Nutrients**. These are substances that build your body's cells, heat and cool your body, and keep you alive.

Macronutrients and **micronutrients** are the major groups of nutrients. Macronutrients are substances that you need to eat in large quantities. They form the foundation of your diet. You need to eat micronutrients too, but you don't need as much of them.

Protein is important because it helps your body grow, repair itself, and maintain healthy cells. It also produces the **hormones** and chemicals that your body needs to survive. Protein is made up of a chain of chemical compounds called amino acids.

WORDS to KNOW

nutrients: substances that strengthen or build up your body.

macronutrients: protein, carbohydrates, and fats needed by the body in relatively large quantities every day.

micronutrients: vitamins and minerals needed by the body in small quantities every day.

protein: one of the basic building blocks of nutrition.

hormones: compounds that work with specific organs in your body.

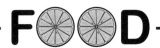
Carbohydrates are your body's main source of energy. When carbohydrates are broken down they yield glucose, a sugar. This is what gives you energy.

Some carbohydrates convert to sugar faster than others. For example, carbohydrates like white sugars break down very rapidly, producing a quick surge of energy. Unfortunately, once you burn off that energy, you'll feel ready to fall asleep. For this reason, nutrition experts recommend that you eat more complex carbohydrates, like whole grains and beans, which release energy more gradually.

carbohydrates: one of the basic building blocks of nutrition, that give you energy.

essential fatty acids: necessary substances found in fish and some plants that your body can't make on its own.

dehydration: dangerous loss of body fluids.

Remember the story about the race between the turtle and the hare? You want to eat carbohydrates that will burn at a slow and steady pace, like the turtle's, not lightening quick, like the hare's. This way you'll feel full for longer and have energy throughout the whole day.

Fats are often presented as the "bad guys" in nutrition. If you eat too many fats, you can end up overweight and unhealthy. However, you do need some fats in your diet. Why? Because fats give your body some vitamins and **essential fatty acids**. These lubricate joints, fight infection, regulate oxygen use, and maintain mental sharpness.

Vitamins are substances that your body needs for many different purposes. They help your body maintain healthy red blood cells, as well as absorb calcium, heal wounds, digest food, and protect sharp vision.

Minerals are chemical compounds like calcium, sodium, and zinc. Your body needs these for blood circulation, bone growth, and hormone production, among other functions.

Getting What You Need

The best way to give your body the energy it needs is to eat a variety of natural foods. Stay away from processed foods, such as frozen meals, snacks, and sodas. Processed foods tend to have less of the nutrients that your body needs.

IN ADDITION TO PROTEIN, CARBOHYDRATES, FATS, VITAMINS, AND MINERALS, YOU ALSO NEED TO CONSUME A FEW OTHER THINGS EVERY DAY.

NUTRIENT . . . FOUND IN

Protein . . . Meat, beans, eggs, dairy products, soybeans

Carbohydrates . . . Pasta, bread, potatoes, beans, rice

Fats . . . Fish, seeds, nuts, oils

Vitamins . . . Fruits, vegetables, milk, cereal

Minerals . . . Eggs, salt, bananas, potato skins

Water is critical to your health. While you can live for weeks without food, you'd face **dehydration** and death in a matter of days without water. Many foods contain some water, but eating them is no substitute for just drinking water. You need water to carry out basic body functions and to maintain your cells, which are primarily composed of water.

Dietary fiber comes from plants. It helps your body digest and get rid of waste. There are two types of fiber: soluble and insoluble. Soluble fiber slows down the digestive process.

F⬤D

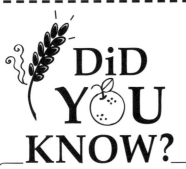

DiD YOU KNOW?

There are two main kinds of vitamins. One kind can't be stored in your body so you need it every day (like Vitamins B and C). The other can be stored (like Vitamins A and K).

The extra time allows more nutrients to enter your body. Soluble fiber also helps your body maintain the right amount of cholesterol. Oats, beans, nuts, and seeds all contain soluble fiber.

Insoluble fiber bulks foods up and helps them move through your intestines more smoothly. You get this kind of fiber from eating vegetables and whole grains.

ONE GRAM OF . . . HAS

Protein . . . 4 calories

Carbohydrate . . . 4 calories

Fat . . . 9 calories

Calories

People usually mention the word "calories" when they are dieting. "I can't eat that," they may say. "It's got too many calories." However, you need calories to live.

So what is a calorie? A calorie is a unit of energy. To be more precise, it is the amount of energy required to raise the temperature of 1 gram of water 1 degree Celsius (slightly less than 2 degrees Fahrenheit). Different nutrients have different amounts of calories, because they require different amounts of energy to "burn" them. It takes more energy to burn one gram of fat than it does to burn one gram of protein.

Kids should consume 1,600 to 2,500 calories a day. Why the range? Because there are many factors that affect how many calories you need per day. It depends on your age, body type, and current level of activity. If you eat more calories than your body needs, you will gain weight. If you eat less calories than your body needs, you will lose weight. Losing weight too quickly or in the wrong way can make you sick.

A Pyramid the Egyptians Didn't Build . . .

To stay healthy, you should eat a "balanced diet." But what is a balanced diet and how do you know you're eating one?

In 1992, the United States Department of Agriculture (USDA) came up with a way to show people what they should be eating. The food pyramid separates food into groups. It then suggests how much of each food group you should be eating every day:

- Bread, rice, pasta, cereal: 6–11 servings
- Vegetables: 3–5 servings
- Fruits: 2–4 servings
- Dairy products: 2–3 servings
- Meat, fish, eggs, beans, nuts: 2–3 servings
- Fats, oils, sugars: "sparingly"

There's also the "Healthy Eating Pyramid," created more recently by the Department of Nutrition at the Harvard School of Public Health. This pyramid is a little different from that of the USDA. It includes other aspects of a healthy life, like exercise and multivitamins. It also suggests:

- Whole grains at most meals
- Regular consumption of plant oils, like olive and sunflower seed oil
- More than 3 servings of vegetables daily
- 2–3 servings of fruit daily
- 1–3 servings of nuts daily
- 1–2 servings of dairy daily
- 1–2 servings of poultry, fish, or eggs daily
- White rice, white bread, red meat, and butter used only "sparingly"

DiD YOU KNOW?

Legumes (like peas and beans) and bran have the most fiber of any plant.

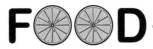

But what is a "serving"? You might be surprised by the size of an actual serving, because we're so used to seeing huge portions on our plates at restaurants and in advertising.

A SERVING OF . . . IS THE SIZE OF A

Meat, fish, or poultry . . . Deck of cards

Dried fruit or nuts . . . Golf ball

Cheese . . . 6 dice

Baked potato . . . Computer mouse

Oatmeal, cereal, pasta . . . Tennis ball

Mayonnaise . . . 1 die

Cream cheese . . . 3 dice

Cookies . . . Top of a soda can

Fruit, vegetables . . . Baseball

Which Food Pyramid Is Right?

Some people think the USDA's food pyramid is too general. For example, it puts all grains together into one group. The Healthy Eating Pyramid divides grains up into whole grains, which keep you satisfied longer, and refined grains, which give you quick, but short-lasting, energy.

THE USDA'S PYRAMID GROUPS ALL MEAT TOGETHER WHILE THE HEALTHY PYRAMID DISTINGUISHES BETWEEN RED MEAT AND LEAN PROTEIN LIKE POULTRY, FISH, AND EGGS.

Finally, the USDA's pyramid puts oils all in the same group, and suggests eating them sparingly. However, as the Healthy Eating Pyramid recognizes, some oils are necessary for your health.

Diet and Disease

Will eating a balanced diet filled with wholesome foods guarantee you perfect health? No, but it will increase the odds in your favor. Researchers have made many connections between poor diets and certain diseases.

- Diets high in **saturated fat** can contribute to heart disease.
- High-**sodium** diets can increase the risk of high blood pressure.
- Lack of calcium can lead to **osteoporosis**.

On the flip side, a well-chosen diet can boost your health:

- A high-fiber diet may help prevent cancers like colon and breast cancer and also reduce the chance of heart disease.
- Diets rich in fruits and vegetables may also help prevent some cancers.

WORDS to KNOW

saturated fat: the fat that is the main cause of high blood cholesterol from what you eat. Butter and coconut oil have high amounts of saturated fat.

sodium: found in salt.

osteoporosis: loss of bone density.

DiD YoU KNOW?

Some people believe the agricultural industries have put political pressure on the USDA to promote their foods in the USDA pyramid. These industries don't want people eating less of their particular product.

Blue Zones

Do you know many people who are over 100 years old? Probably not. But there are some places in the world where people routinely break that age barrier. Adventurer and researcher Dan Buettner identified five areas in the world where people have unusually long, healthy lives. He calls these places the "blue zones." The areas are:

- Icara, Greece
- Loma Linda, California
- Nicoya Peninsula, Costa Rica
- Okinawa, Japan
- Sardinia, Italy

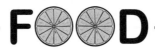

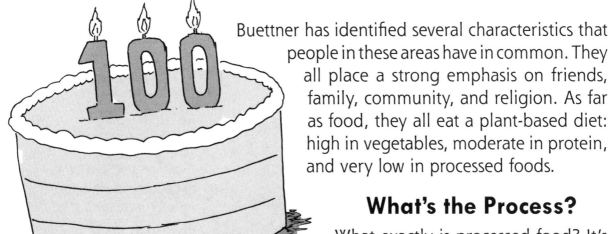

Buettner has identified several characteristics that people in these areas have in common. They all place a strong emphasis on friends, family, community, and religion. As far as food, they all eat a plant-based diet: high in vegetables, moderate in protein, and very low in processed foods.

What's the Process?

What exactly is processed food? It's a food that has undergone changes from its natural state. For instance, an apple is a whole, natural food. However, if you take that apple and transform it into apple pie filling in a can or apple-flavored sugar cereal, it becomes processed.

WHEN YOU ADD CHEMICALS TO FOOD, SUCH AS PRESERVATIVES THAT EXTEND A FOOD'S LONGEVITY, IT BECOMES PROCESSED FOOD.

On the plus side, processed food tends to last longer, decreasing the chance that it will go bad during its journey to the store or while it is sitting on your shelves. On the negative side, processing can reduce the nutritional value of food.

Processed foods are things like:

- Packaged cookies
- Sugar cereals
- Snack foods with lots of calories, such as chips
- Canned meats or deli meat
- Convenience foods, such as frozen dinners

MAKE YOUR OWN
SERVING REMINDER PLATE

Giving your body the right foods to eat is important. But so is portion control. This reminder plate gives you and your family a visual way to remember how much is really enough.

1 Find the objects that represent serving sizes for a variety of foods. Check the chart on page 80.

2 Using the marker or pen, label each object. If it's a golf ball, for example, write "one serving of nuts" on it. For the deck of cards, write "one serving of fish."

3 Cut half-inch pieces of Velcro tape and attach one side of the tape to each of the serving size objects. Attach the other sides of the tape to the plate.

Supplies

- assorted "serving size" objects, such as a tennis ball, deck of cards, and golf ball
- marker or pen
- scissors
- sticky Velcro tape
- large paper plate

4 At each meal, attach the serving size objects that match what you're eating. Put the plate where you and your family can see it easily. Before long, you'll all have a great idea of what a serving size looks like for many foods!

83

MAKE YOUR OWN DECK OF
SUBSTITUTIONS CARDS

Supplies

- colored paper
- scissors
- pen or marker
- tape
- stack of index cards
- envelope

Eating a nutritionally balanced diet doesn't have to be blah or boring. Create this "deck of substitutions" cards and you can deal out healthy, tasty swaps for foods you already enjoy.

1 Using the colored paper, cut small "tabs" for your cards. Label each one with a food category that will make sense to you. You could use "Dairy," "Meats," "Snacks," and so on.

2 Tape one tab to the top (along the long side) of each index card. You may want to stagger them so you can read them easier without flipping through all the cards.

3 Start filling out the swaps on the cards. You can do one substitution per card or several on one card, however you'd like. The list below should get you started.

4 As you come across more substitutions, either online or in books, add them to your card deck.

5 Keep them in the kitchen for when your family is cooking, or in the car for when you go to the grocery store.

INSTEAD OF . . . TRY

cookies . . . graham crackers, fig bars, ginger snaps (or make your own low-calorie/low-fat version)

donuts, muffins . . . English muffins, bagels

pound cake, chocolate cake . . . angel food cake, gingerbread

cream cheese . . . Neufchatel, "light" cream cheese

whole milk . . . Skim, low-fat, reduced-fat milk

butter . . . light margarine, spray butter

pasta with white sauce . . . pasta with red sauce

oil . . . applesauce in baked goods

ice cream . . . sherbet, sorbet, frozen yogurt

sour cream . . . plain low-fat yogurt

white rice . . . brown rice

hot dogs . . . turkey dogs

tuna in oil . . . tuna in water

ground beef . . . ground turkey, extra lean ground beef

bacon . . . Canadian bacon

hot fudge . . . chocolate syrup

processed guacamole . . . salsa

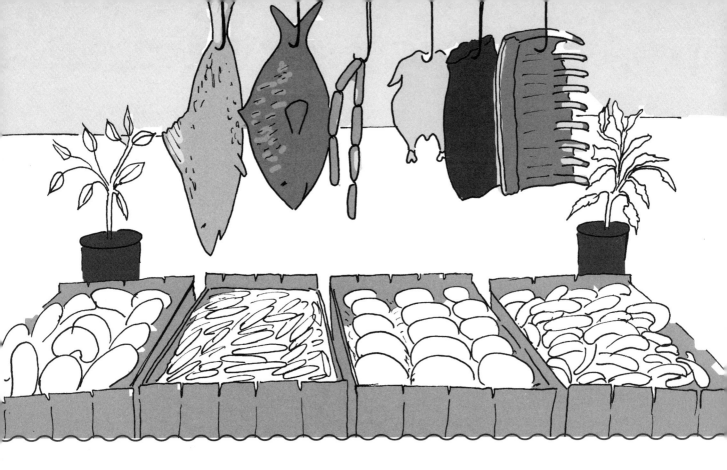

"MEAT" ME AT
THE VEGGIE STAND

Most animals eat only a few foods. Sharks? They eat mostly fish or seals. Pandas? Almost all their diet is bamboo. Koalas eat eucalyptus leaves, cows eat grasses and grains, and robins eat insects and worms.

If you tried to list what people eat, you'd have a much more difficult time. Humans eat a wide range of foods, everything from meat and vegetables to fruits and grains.

WORDS to KNOW

herbivore: an animal that eats only plants.

carnivore: an animal that eats other animals.

omnivore: an animal that eats both plants and animals.

digestive tract: the passage between the mouth and the anus, including the stomach and other organs that food passes through for digestion and elimination as waste.

prey: an animal caught or hunted for food.

But what are humans designed to eat? Are we **herbivores**, who eat a plant-based diet, **carnivores**, who eat a meat-based diet, or **omnivores**, who eat both.

IT'S SIMPLE TO TELL WHETHER AN ANIMAL IS AN HERBIVORE, CARNIVORE, OR OMNIVORE. BIOLOGISTS JUST LOOK AT THE DIGESTIVE TRACT. THIS TELLS THEM WHAT TYPE OF FOOD AN ANIMAL IS ABLE TO BREAK DOWN SO ITS BODY CAN ACCESS THE NUTRIENTS.

Herbivores have a long **digestive tract** to break down plant material. Plant material can remain in their digestive tract for some time so that it can be fully digested. Herbivores have very wide, flat teeth that start the process of breaking down plant material in their mouths. They also have an enzyme in their saliva to help digest tough plant cells.

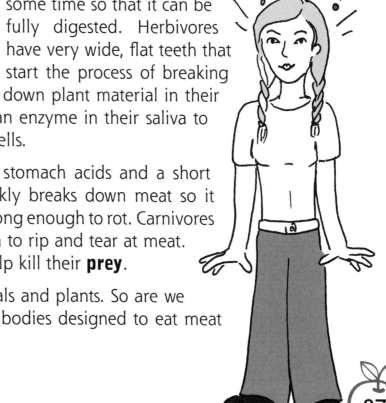

Carnivores have strong stomach acids and a short digestive tract. This quickly breaks down meat so it doesn't stay inside them long enough to rot. Carnivores have sharp, pointed teeth to rip and tear at meat. These sharp teeth also help kill their **prey**.

Humans eat both animals and plants. So are we true omnivores? Are our bodies designed to eat meat and plants?

Like herbivores, we have flat teeth that are close together. However, like carnivores, we struggle to digest foods like grass or raw wheat, because we lack the special enzyme that herbivores have for this process. Sometimes we also have difficulty digesting raw vegetables and beans, too.

The length of our digestive tract falls somewhere between the very short one of a true carnivore's, such as a cat's, and the very long one of a true herbivore's, such as a cow's.

So if you look at the design of our bodies, it makes sense that we are true omnivores, who can eat meat and many plants.

DiD YOU KNOW?

A cow's stomach has four compartments to process the plants it eats.

FILLING YOUR PLATE

Some people choose not to eat meat at all. They become **vegetarians**. They make this decision for many different reasons. They might stop eating meat for **ethical** reasons, such as being morally opposed to eating other animals. Or they might become vegetarians for health reasons, believing that plant-based diets are better for their bodies. Maybe they believe it's better for the environment. There are also religious reasons for choosing not to eat meat.

Whatever the reason, most vegetarians primarily eat fruits, vegetables, grains, nuts, and seeds.

THERE ARE NO STRICT RULES ABOUT BEING A VEGETARIAN. SOME VEGETARIANS SIMPLY DON'T EAT RED MEAT. SOME EAT POULTRY OR FISH OCCASIONALLY, WHILE OTHERS NEVER DO, OR THEY CONSUME EGGS, BUT ALWAYS REFUSE FISH.

Within vegetarianism, there are groups of people who are even more specific about what they can and cannot eat. **Vegans**, for example, reject any products that come from animals, including dairy, eggs, and honey. They may also refuse to wear animal-based clothing, such as leather, wool, or down items.

Vegetarianism isn't a new way of life. It's been around since ancient times. Some famous vegetarians in history include:

- **Pythagoras**, the Greek mathematician and philosopher
- **Plato**, the Greek philosopher
- **Leonardo da Vinci**, the Italian painter and architect
- **Sir Isaac Newton**, the English physicist and mathematician
- **Benjamin Franklin**, the American scientist
- **Charlotte Bronte**, the English author
- **Henry Ford**, the American car maker
- **Albert Einstein**, the Swiss-German scientist

Some countries generally eat a more plant-based diet than Americans. This may be because meat is very expensive in these areas. It's also because of ancient tradition. For many Asian people, noodles or rice form the main part of the meal, while soy products, such as tofu and miso, are also very important.

WORDS to KNOW

vegetarian: someone who eats a plant-based diet.

ethical: acting in a way that upholds someone's belief in right and wrong.

vegan: a vegetarian who won't eat anything that comes from an animal, like dairy or eggs.

Meanwhile, in the Mediterranean, people eat large quantities of pasta, bread, cheese, and vegetables. In India, fruits, vegetables, **legumes**, and flatbreads dominate the menu. Central and South American meals are based on beans and tortillas.

WORDS to KNOW

legumes: plants with seeds that grow in pods, like peas and beans.

antioxidant: a substance in food that helps fight disease.

fortified: when a food has nutrients added to it.

GETTING THE GOODS

So can you stay healthy eating a vegetarian diet? Generally, diets rich in plant-based foods are low in fat and high in fiber, which is good. Fruits and vegetables also supply many vitamins, minerals, and **antioxidants**, which help fight diseases like cancer.

However, vegetarians need to be aware of what's missing in a meatless diet. To fill in any gaps in nutrition that might develop as a result of their restricted diets, vegetarians need to make sure to eat certain foods to get enough vitamins and minerals.

DiD YOU KNOW?

One fast food chain sells around 5 million hamburgers every day.

NEED TO KISS YOUR BURGER GOOD-BYE?

With care you can obtain all the nutrients you need from a vegetarian diet. So should you stop eating meat right now? Not necessarily. Before you make any changes in your diet, you should do your own research, explore all of your options, and reach your own conclusions.

NUTRITION EXPERTS AGREE THAT REDUCING THE AMOUNT OF RED MEAT IN YOUR DIET IS A HEALTHY CHOICE.

CALCIUM. If you don't eat dairy products, you must find another source of calcium. This essential mineral helps build strong bones and teeth, move muscles, and keep nerves functioning.

WHERE TO GET IT: Greens like kale, broccoli, and turnip greens are a good source of calcium. Some juices and cereals are also **fortified** with calcium.

VITAMIN B12. Unfortunately for vegans, animal products are the only natural source of this vitamin. B12 assists the normal functioning of the brain and nervous system.

WHERE TO GET IT: Vegans can use vitamin supplements to get enough B12 in their diets, while other vegetarians can eat dairy products and eggs.

VITAMIN D. Time in the sun gives you Vitamin D, which helps your bones and teeth absorb calcium. If you wear sunscreen or live in a northern or cloudy environment, you'll need to add extra Vitamin D to your diet.

WHERE TO GET IT: Milk is fortified with Vitamin D, as are some cereals.

VITAMIN C. Humans also need Vitamin C, a substance that helps boost your immune system and aids in the absorption of iron.

WHERE TO GET IT: Citrus fruits such as oranges, grapefruit, and lemons. Strawberries, kiwi, and broccoli are also all excellent sources of vitamin C.

IRON. This mineral helps your blood transport oxygen around your body. If your body doesn't have enough iron, you'll feel sluggish and weak.

WHERE TO GET IT: Broccoli, spinach, and seeds are good sources of iron. Whole grains and iron-fortified foods are great ways to get iron, too.

WORDS to KNOW

free-range: animals who are allowed to graze in open areas instead of being confined to an enclosure.

pharmaceuticals: drugs used for medications.

humanely: treating a living creature with compassion.

The decision to eat or not to eat red meat can be a controversial one, with animal rights and environmental activists squaring off against people in the beef industry, for example.

Why? Just as farming has moved from small-scale farming to mega-farming, so has the raising of livestock. Today, most chickens and pigs are raised in massive metal buildings. Most cattle spend their last months in giant pens called feedyards. For this reason, many people prefer buying their meat from small farms with **free-range** animals that are slaughtered on an as-needed basis.

PEOPLE WORRY ABOUT THE CONDITIONS IN WHICH ANIMALS ARE RAISED, AS WELL AS THE WAYS IN WHICH THEY ARE KILLED.

Other people are concerned about the large amounts of grain used to feed these animals. They argue that it would make more economic and environmental sense for people to eat more grain than meat, that the land taken up by raising livestock could be better used to grow more crops. But is it always possible to grow crops on the land used to raise animals? Not necessarily.

DiD YOU KNOW?

People in the livestock industry don't like the idea of consumers cutting back their meat consumption. Selling meat is how they earn their living.

And what are the alternative plant-based sources of protein? Tofu is highly refined and requires large amounts of farmland, perhaps more than what is needed to raise meat. The issues are complicated with no easy answers.

There are many people who are concerned about hormones and other **pharmaceuticals** given to the animals to increase their growth and production. They are afraid that these chemicals will make their way into the systems of the people who eat the meat of these animals.

What if you just can't bring yourself to stop eating hamburgers, or pepperoni on your pizza? How can you eat meat and still help animals and the environment? One option is to support local farmers. Another is to only buy meat from free-range animals that were treated **humanely**.

When planning your diet, remember that it's most important to be aware of what you're putting into your body. Then you can make your own choices about the food that works best for you.

93

BACKYARD EATING

You've learned that food production, processing, and packaging has changed dramatically over time. Advances in transportation, including trains, cargo ships, and airplanes, allowed farmers to ship crops thousands of miles away.

With these advances in transportation, people could eat foods that they had never tried, or even heard of, before! Shipments of regional, seasonal, and tropical foods started to crisscross the globe.

94

WORDS to KNOW

environmentalist: someone who works to preserve the environment.

greenhouse gases: carbon monoxide and other gases that get into the atmosphere and trap heat.

locavore: someone who eats foods grown locally, whenever possible.

Oranges, once a special winter treat for people in warm climates, have become an everyday breakfast food that is widely available. Now you can find jars of Brazil nuts or bananas from Chile in your local supermarket. While it's incredible to have access to new flavors, there is a downside to shipments of food moving all over the world.

Environmentalists are concerned about **greenhouse gases** produced by the planes, ships, trains, and trucks used to transport food from distant locations to your supermarket. They are also worried about the chemicals used in food production on large farms.

SOME PEOPLE WORRY THAT SCIENTISTS WILL EVENTUALLY DISCOVER THAT MANY CHEMICALS WE THINK ARE SAFE ARE ACTUALLY HARMFUL, IN THE LONG RUN.

THE NEIGHBORLY WAY TO EAT

Today, more and more people are thinking about where their food comes from. Some have made a decision to buy some, if not all, of their food from local suppliers. Through their actions, these **locavores** are trying to reduce the environmental pollution produced by mega-farming and long-distance transportation of foods.

DiD YOU KNOW?

All coffee is grown within 1,000 miles of the equator—so it's shipped quite a distance to get to many coffee-lovers!

95

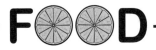

WORDS to KNOW

organic: food grown or raised according to certain standards, without artificial fertilizers, perticides, or hormones.

fertilizers: something added to soil to make it more fertile.

Most people think the taste of local produce is superior. You read about how ethylene gas naturally ripens fruits and vegetables. Local farmers pick their produce after it has released ethylene and ripened on the vine. This creates a better flavor. Large-scale commercial farmers pick their produce before it ripens on the vine, so it won't spoil on the trip to your supermarket. This reduces its flavor.

WHERE'D THAT COME FROM?

Chances are, you don't know where the food in your grocery store is from. Your produce might have a little sticker saying "Product of Chile," but that's about all the information you'll get. Often, you won't know *how* the food was made either. Did the farmer or manufacturer use pesticides or additives?

For these reasons, many people prefer buying **organic** food. Usually, organic fruits and vegetables are grown without chemical pesticides or chemical **fertilizers**. Organic livestock eat a healthy diet without growth hormones. The animals graze in open spaces, rather than being kept in confined areas.

ORGANIC AGRICULTURE IS A RETURN TO FARMING THAT USES NATURALLY PRODUCED FERTILIZERS AND NO CHEMICALS. THIS PROTECTS THE ENVIRONMENT AND PRODUCES HEALTHIER, BETTER-TASTING FOOD.

Organic produce doesn't always look as perfect as commercial produce, but organic food lovers claim that it wins on taste. Unfortunately, organic food tends to be more expensive because it costs more to produce food organically.

JUMPING IN

You can bring together locavores in your area by constructing a community garden. Find a plot of land big enough for a good-sized vegetable garden. Make sure everyone has access to it. Then have a meeting where everyone discusses what they can contribute. You want to get everyone involved in planting, tending, and harvesting the crops. Then set up a work schedule so everyone knows their responsibilities. If you get everyone working together, you can create a really amazing garden!

GONNA GARDEN?

The only thing that tastes better than fresh produce from the farmer's market is fresh produce straight from your own garden! Using raised beds provides elevated areas where plants can grow, keeping the soil warm and fighting weeds. First put down thick layers of newspaper to block the weeds. Pile a foot or more of soil on top. You can keep it from spreading out by building a border of wood around it. Weeds and grass will have a tough time getting through the newspaper. Take the time to plan a garden layout that will offer you the best chance of success:

- Pick a location that receives lots of sun.
- Place raised beds in a north–south direction, to prevent the plants from shading each other.
- Plant tall plants like corn, beans, and peas on the north side of the garden so they don't block sunlight from the other plants.
- Plant mid-sized plants like tomatoes, squash, cauliflower, and pumpkins next.
- Fill the last section with short plants like radishes, onions, carrots, and lettuce.

DiD YOU KNOW?

The most popular produce grown in backyard gardens includes tomatoes and cucumbers.

MAKE YOUR OWN
FARMER'S MARKET SURVEY

Is there really a difference between locally grown, small-farm produce and the commercial produce you buy in a large supermarket? Take this fun survey with your family to find out!

Supplies

- commercial fruits and vegetables from a large supermarket, and the same types of local produce from the farmer's market
- pen or pencil
- paper for survey
- plates
- kitchen knife
- blindfold (optional)

1 Buy enough produce so everyone in your family can sample everything.

2 Create a survey form with three columns labeled: Name of produce, Farmer's market, and Supermarket. Set out two plates labeled on the bottom: "A" for commercial produce and "B" for local produce.

3 Wash each type of produce and cut it into small pieces. Put the commercial sample on one plate and the local sample on the other plate.

4 The tasters should not know which piece is local and which piece is commercial. So blindfold them if they can tell them apart by sight. Have the tasters sample each piece and tell you which they prefer.

5 On the survey form, put a check under each tester's preference for each piece. After all the produce has been tasted, check to see which column has the greatest number of votes.

MAKE YOUR OWN
HOME-GROWN
VEGETABLE SAMPLER

If your yard space is limited, try this unique tomato garden.

1 Place your straw bale on a stable, flat surface. With an adult's help, use the hand saw to cut two large, round holes into the top of the bale. Don't cut all the way through the bale, and also avoid cutting the twine that's holding the bale together. The bales will fall apart and make a big mess if you cut the twine!

2 Fill the holes halfway with potting soil and mix in some fertilizer. Carefully remove the tomato plants from their pots and place them in the holes. Gently pack some more potting soil around them.

3 Put the bale in a place that gets plenty of sunlight. Water as needed. Soon, you should have delicious tomatoes growing on the vine!

Supplies

- bale of straw
- small hand saw
- potting soil
- organic fertilizer
- tomato plants

YOU'RE EATING WHAT?!

Imagine you're at a buffet. You're starving and can't wait to eat! As you read the descriptions of the food, however, your appetite starts to fade: fried tarantulas, live oysters, sheep's head, dog meat, and even chalky white clay. What's going on? Where's the pizza, the spaghetti, the fruit salad?

People around the world can have very different ideas about what foods are appetizing. You might be grossed out by the idea of eating fried grasshoppers. But in parts of Africa, Asia, and the Middle East, they're a quick, crunchy snack. During pioneer times, Americans boiled locusts in soup! Before you decide to become an insectivore, remember, never eat anything before checking with a responsible adult first!

If eating bugs sounds disgusting, keep in mind that some foods you eat might be equally appalling to people in other cultures. For many people in India, for example, the idea of eating a beef hamburger would be shocking. They believe that all animal life is sacred. In particular, they honor cows as highly sacred beasts, treating them with care and allowing them to roam freely.

THE MCDONALD'S RESTAURANTS IN INDIA SERVE A VARIETY OF MEATLESS BURGERS INSTEAD OF BEEF!

Even in the United States, there are popular foods in certain areas that might seem pretty gross to some people:

Scrapple: Some people in Delaware, Pennsylvania, Maryland, and New Jersey make scrapple from scraps of pork and cornmeal. These parts, which include bones, are boiled together to produce a jelly-like substance that is formed into a loaf, sliced, and fried. When we say someone is "scrappy," we are using a word that comes down to us from when making scrapple was common on American farms.

Geoduck Clams: Found in the Pacific Northwest, these large clams can weigh up to 2 pounds. They have long, tongue-like "siphons" that extend out approximately 3 feet past their shell! Geoduck clams are served raw, in sushi, or cooked in chowder.

Crawfish: In the coastal South, people eat crawfish, which look like miniature lobsters. People pull the heads from the cooked crawfish and suck the fat out of the heads. Then they pull the meat out of the bodies to eat it.

Grits: Throughout most of the South, people eat grits with their meals. Grits consist of boiled coarse cornmeal with cheese, butter, or even sugar. Some people also eat chitterlings, or chitlins, which are fried pig intestines.

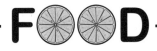

ABOUT THOSE BUGS...

People eat insects all over the world. Why? For starters, they're free! And they live everywhere.

Insects are also a surprisingly good source of protein. Every 100 grams of caterpillar yields about 53 grams of protein. This compares to only 28 grams of protein for every 100 grams of beef, which is about one hamburger patty.

While spiders aren't really insects, they're often associated with insects. Spiders are arachnids. If you like lobster or crab, you might think twice about refusing to eat spiders or scorpions. Lobster and crab are arachnids, too!

DiD Y U KNOW?

In an extreme situation, eating insects can save your life. In 2004, U.S. Air Force fighter pilot Scott O'Grady's plane was shot down in enemy territory in Bosnia. He survived on a diet that included ants. In 2008, an injured climber in Washington State survived by eating centipedes, ants, and even a venomous wolf spider.

DiD Y U KNOW?

People eat deep-fried tarantula in parts of Cambodia!

LIKE INSECTS, PEOPLE ALL OVER THE WORLD EAT FLOWERS.

STOP AND EAT THE FLOWERS

Daisies, pansies, roses, lilacs, violets, and sunflowers are used to create dishes that are fragrant, flavorful, and pretty to look at, too. Of course, not all flowers are edible, and some are even dangerous to consume.

Rats! Dinner Just Got Away

Although we may think of rodents as dirty critters, they're dinner in many cultures. In South America, ancient people raised guinea pigs for food. They are still eaten regularly there. Meanwhile, the ancient Romans ate dormice, roasted and dipped in honey. Rats make up half of the locally produced meat consumed in the Africa country of Ghana. And in parts of the southern United States, people often hunt and eat squirrels.

Some flowers are full of vitamins and minerals. The lowly dandelion, considered an annoying weed throughout much of America, packs a surprising nutritional punch.

One cup of dandelion leaves gives you 112 percent of your daily recommended dose of vitamin A and over 500 percent of the recommended allowance of vitamin K. The leaves are also rich in Vitamin C, potassium, calcium, and iron.

Some people roast and grind dandelion roots as a coffee substitute. Others fry the flowers and buds to eat. Dandelion flowers make excellent wine. Some cultures use dandelions for medicinal purposes, believing that they work to cleanse the liver and reduce inflammation.

THAT WAS THEN, THIS IS NOW

Foods come in and out of fashion. Today, for example, people eat much less butter than they once did, because of health concerns.

There are also foods that we eat today that people in the past refused to eat. For example, in colonial America most people thought tomatoes were poisonous.

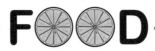
In 1820, the attitude towards tomatoes changed. According to legend, Colonel Robert Gibbon Johnson stood on the steps of the courthouse in Salem, Massachusetts, and ate an entire basket of tomatoes. Since he didn't fall violently ill or die, people began to accept that tomatoes were safe to eat.

People also once shunned oats, believing that they were only suitable for horses. Today, people recognize oat products as an important part of a healthy diet.

Shark Fin Soup

Shark fin soup is a luxury dish in Asia. The main ingredient is, of course, shark fins. The problem is that many sharks are killed during the harvesting process, as fishermen slice off the fins and then toss the sharks back into the ocean to sink to the bottom and die.

THE COST OF YOUR MEAL

Sometimes, human demand for exotic foods can place the environment at risk. For example, in Asia, one highly valued culinary treat is bird's nest soup. As the name suggests, this soup is made from the nests of certain birds that live in bat-filled caves.

The birds make their nests by weaving seaweed, twigs, moss, hair, and feathers. Then they cement the nests together with their saliva. These nests are hard to reach and it takes a lot of skill and experience to harvest them. As a result, the price of a bowl of bird's nest soup can run around $300!

Unfortunately, every time a nest is harvested, the birds must rebuild another nest before they can lay their eggs.

MAKE YOUR OWN
BUG FEAST

When you think about it, it's not any stranger to eat insects than to eat the odd-looking lobster. Here's a fun way to teach friends and family that other people really do eat insects!

Ants on a log

1 Wash and dry the celery stalks and dry them thoroughly.

2 Spread peanut butter or cream cheese onto the celery.

3 Sprinkle the raisin "ants" over the celery "log."

Supplies

- celery
- peanut butter or cream cheese
- knife
- raisins

Caterpillars

1 Peel the banana and cut it into slices. Stick all the slices together in a row with the peanut butter to form the caterpillar body. Set aside.

2 Gently poke pretzel sticks side-by-side into the top of the grape. The pretzel sticks are the antennae.

3 Attach the grape head to one end of the caterpillar with the peanut butter. You can also attach pairs of short pretzel sticks to each banana section for legs.

Supplies

- banana
- knife
- peanut butter
- thin pretzel sticks
- grape

MAKE YOUR OWN
FRIED DANDELION BLOSSOMS

Ready to try eating dandelions? First, pick them from a place that you know hasn't been sprayed with chemicals. And don't gather them from beside a road, since they can easily pick up pollutants there. Wash the dandelions thoroughly. You will need an adult to help with the frying.

1 Choose fresh blossoms that are young and bright yellow in color, with no wispy seeds.

2 Trim off the stems as close as you possibly can to the blossoms. The stems are very bitter, so you don't want to eat them.

3 Wash the blossoms, and then thoroughly dry them by wrapping them in paper towels. The drier they are, the easier they'll be to batter and fry.

Supplies

- 2–3 cups yellow dandelion blossoms
- paper towels
- mixing bowls and spoons
- 1 egg
- 1 cup milk
- 1 cup flour
- 1 teaspoon salt
- 1 teaspoon pepper
- small frying pan
- vegetable oil

4 Beat together the egg and milk. In a separate bowl, mix together the dry ingredients, then whisk them into the egg and milk mixture.

5 In a small frying pan, heat some oil to approximately 350–375 degrees Fahrenheit (175–190 degrees Celsius).

6 Dip the dry blossoms into the batter, and then fry them immediately.

7 When the blossoms have turned a light brown color, lift them out of the oil and drain on paper towels.

8 Eat the blossoms as soon as they're cool enough to handle.

THE FUTURE OF FOOD

When you think about the future, what comes to mind? Hovercrafts taking you to school and soccer practice? Holographic movies that project into the middle of your living room? Smell-o-vision television shows?

Some of our food is unchanged from the past. For example, we're still eating dried meat—like jerky—the same way ancient people did.

But other things have changed quite a lot over time. Today we make popcorn in a microwave instead of over a fire. We eat oranges year round.

Changes have usually improved our food production and even our health. But some changes have put the future of our food at risk, too. Some of the chemicals we've used to grow crops are hurting our environment. These are some of the issues that farmers, scientists, and consumers need to think about.

What will food look and taste like in the future? As we continue to develop new technologies, we will gain new opportunities to alter food.

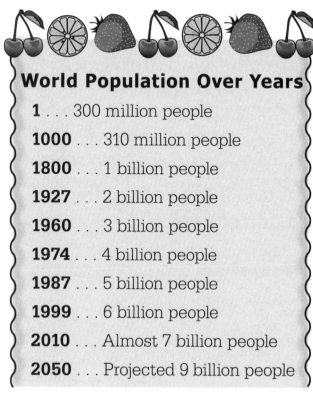

World Population Over Years

1 . . . 300 million people

1000 . . . 310 million people

1800 . . . 1 billion people

1927 . . . 2 billion people

1960 . . . 3 billion people

1974 . . . 4 billion people

1987 . . . 5 billion people

1999 . . . 6 billion people

2010 . . . Almost 7 billion people

2050 . . . Projected 9 billion people

WE MIGHT LEARN TO CREATE NEW FOOD. OR "IMPROVE" EXISTING FOODS WITH CHEMICALS OR HIGH-TECH GROWING METHODS.

As the population grows, demand for food will continue to rise. This will put pressure on farmers to produce more food faster. Unfortunately, there's only a limited amount of space for food production, and it can only happen so fast. Something's got to give.

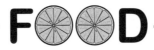

F**O**O**D

WORKING THE LAND

Farmers know that growing the same crop over and over in the same soil depletes its nutrients. So they add fertilizers to the soil or to the plants themselves to help them grow bigger, faster, and healthier.

Some fertilizers, like peat, are natural, while others are artificial and produced in the laboratory. If fertilizers are used correctly, they can replenish lost nutrients in the soil. However, if too much fertilizer is added to the soil, **leaching** can occur.

LEACHING TAKES PLACE WHEN THE SOIL IS UNABLE TO ACCEPT THE EXTRA NUTRIENTS IN THE FERTILIZER. THE UNABSORBED CHEMICAL NUTRIENTS RUN OFF WITH THE RAIN AND ENTER THE water cycle, WHERE THEY CAN HARM OTHER ORGANISMS.

Some fertilizer contains **nitrogen**. Too much nitrogen ends up contributing to the **greenhouse effect**. The greenhouse effect describes what happens when the atmosphere above the earth becomes so thick with gases that it traps heat.

While fertilizers may make fruits and vegetables look better, some people feel the produce isn't as tasty or as healthy as naturally grown produce.

Along with water vapor and nitrous oxide (from nitrogen), the greenhouse gases are carbon dioxide, methane, and ozone.

PEST, BE GONE!

One of the biggest problems farmers face is insects and other unwanted pests that can reduce the farm's output. Rodents, insects, fungi, and mites feed on the crops before, and sometimes after, harvest. Pesticides are often used to control and try to eliminate these pests.

One of the problems with pesticides, though, is that they're often toxic to other animals. They also can be harmful to humans.

For example, the chemical DDT (with a full name like dichlorodiphenyltrichloroethane, it's much easier just to go by its initials!) caused a great deal of environmental damage in the past. Governments first started using DDT toward the end of World War II to control mosquitoes that spread **malaria** among the troops, as well as lice that carried **typhus**.

DDT was very effective in killing these insects, and saved an estimated 25 million human lives. It was also cheap. After the war, farmers in the United States began to use it as a pesticide.

By the 1950s, DDT was so widely used that many insects started to develop resistance to it. DDT didn't kill them anymore. Environmental experts began to ask questions about DDT's effect on the environment.

In 2008, 12 countries were still using DDT to protect against malaria.

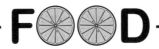

In 1962, naturalist Rachel Carson published a book called *Silent Spring*. This book argued that pesticides like DDT were harming the environment. They were putting wildlife at risk and endangering human health. The book had the same effect on environmentalism as Upton Sinclair's *The Jungle* had on food safety. It sounded a warning bell, loud and clear. As a result, people began to demand change.

NOT A DROP TO DRINK

Without water, you couldn't survive for very long at all. Chances are, you have easy access to all the water you could want to drink. You just turn on the tap at the sink and fill a cup or reach in the refrigerator and grab some bottled water.

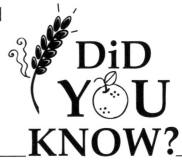

DiD YOU KNOW?

Lack of water not only poses a risk to human life, but also harms the environment. When water **evaporates**, it draws minerals up to the surface. This forms a hard crust that makes it virtually impossible for any food to be grown there.

However, in many parts of the world, getting water is a more difficult and time-consuming endeavor. Sometimes the water is not even safe enough to drink. Nonetheless, the people in these regions of the world may be so desperate for water that they end up drinking it anyway, and come down with potentially deadly diseases like dysentery and cholera.

WATER SHORTAGES SOMETIMES RESULT FROM NATURAL CONDITIONS.

WORDS to KNOW

evaporate: change from a liquid to a gas.

irrigation: any method to water crops.

Some areas are very arid and don't receive a lot of rainfall or have sources of freshwater. Extended periods of drought can also threaten water supplies. Sometimes, however, individuals waste water or choose **irrigation** systems for crops that use water unwisely.

THE WORLD FACES SOME FUTURE CHALLENGES IN REGARD TO BOTH FOOD AND WATER. FORTUNATELY, PLENTY OF PEOPLE ARE WORKING HARD TO FIND SOLUTIONS.

WHAT COMES NEXT?

Since different crops use different nutrients in the soil, crop rotation is one way to keep the soil fertile. In a crop rotation system, farmers grow different types of crops in the same area over time. For example, a farmer might plant cotton one year. Cotton depletes the soil by taking many nutrients from it. So the next year, the farmer might plant peanuts or peas, both crops that enrich the soil.

Another example of crop rotation is:

Year One: Tomatoes/potatoes
Year Two: Squash/corn
Year Three: Legumes
Year Four: Greens

Crop rotation also helps reduce soil erosion, controls pests, and fights against plant diseases. Since it benefits the environment, rotation is one way farmers can continue to grow food for the future.

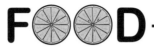

F**O**D

DIRT-FREE FARMING

If you've always wanted to be a farmer but don't like getting dirty, here's the farming of the future for you: **hydroponics**. In hydroponic farming, farmers grow plants in materials other than soil. These materials include gravel, wood fiber, and even sand.

Almost every plant that can be grown in soil can also be grown through hydroponics. Hydroponic gardening is especially beneficial for people who want to grow fresh food in crowded urban areas with no open land.

Aeroponics is another method of soil-free farming. In aeroponic gardening, people hang plants in the air and spray water and nutrients on their roots. These plants grow completely free of any other substance.

WORDS to KNOW

hydroponics: growing plants without soil.

aeroponics: a system of growing plants without any medium for their roots at all.

gravitropism: the ability of plants to detect and grow roots in the direction of gravity.

SPUDS IN SPACE

As Earth gets more crowded, some people think we should expand into space and possibly even other planets. However, this raises an interesting question: What could people eat up there?

FARMSCRAPER

As the world's population expands, the amount of land available for farming shrinks. So farmers in the future may decide to go vertical. Imagine entering a tall skyscraper and riding up a glass elevator. As you travel past floor after floor, you'd see rows and rows of green crops growing strong and healthy.

With vertical farming, farmers grow crops right inside city limits. Using systems like hydroponics or aeroponics, farmers could produce fruits and vegetables year round.

Pill Popping

Plenty of sci-fi flicks have shown the future of food as just a handful of pills. The characters pop some capsules, rub their bellies, and we're supposed to believe that they've just satisfied all their nutritional needs.

Even if you could get all your nutrition from pills, would you really want to? Certainly, taking vitamins and supplements can be part of a healthy diet. However, our bodies tend to perform best when we use whole, natural foods to meet our nutritional needs. Moreover, we very much enjoy the taste, smell, sight, and texture of particular foods. And eating is often a social activity. Researchers have found that eating together as a family helps children do well socially and at school.

You can't just plant crops there. There's no gravity! Here on Earth, plants detect the gravitational field and respond to it by growing roots downward. This is called **gravitropism**. No matter which direction you place a seed into the ground, the plant's roots will always grow downward and shoots will always push upward.

Even if you dig up a growing plant and turn it upside down, the roots will soon begin to grow downward again, while the shoots will turn around and grow upward once more.

But how does a seed in space know which direction to grow? Can it even grow at all? Scientists at the National Air and Space Administration (NASA) are trying to figure this out. Their goal is to be able to grow food for astronauts who are on long missions.

DiD YOU KNOW?

The first vegetable to be grown in space was the potato. In 1995, NASA and the University of Wisconsin-Madison grew a space spud.

MAKE YOUR OWN
BEAN GRAVITY EXPERIMENT

Want to see gravitropism in action? With this experiment, you can watch as a plant figures out which way is really up!

1 In a small cup, plant the bean seed with the potting soil. Water. Wait a few days until the bean seed has sprouted and formed a tiny seedling.

2 Soak the sponges in water until they're completely wet. If they're dripping, wring them out a little bit.

3 Gently remove the bean seedling from the cup. Carefully shake off most of the soil from its roots.

4 Lay the roots of the seedling between the 2 sponges, so that they are sandwiched between them. Make sure the shoot of the plant is sticking out.

5 Tie the sponges together firmly with the string. Use another piece of string to hang the plant upside down in a sunny spot.

6 Check the sponges a few times each day. If they dry out, moisten them with some more water, but don't soak them. You don't want the seedlings' roots to rot.

7 In a few days, the seedling should turn and start to grow upward again, while the roots turn to grow down.

Supplies

- small cup
- potting soil
- bean seed
- 2 sponges
- water
- string

116

MAKE YOUR OWN
SALT FLAT EXPERIMENT

See for yourself how evaporating water can draw minerals up out of the ground. When this happens to the land, it becomes impossible to grow crops there.

1 Pour a layer of salt about a half inch deep onto the bottom of the dish. Cover the salt with about 2 inches of soil. Press down gently to compact the soil.

2 Water the soil until it's thoroughly wet, but not drenched.

3 Place the dish in a warm, sunny place, and check on it every day or two. Whenever it dries out, repeat step 2. Do this for two weeks.

4 Before you water the soil each time, check the surface of the soil with a magnifying glass. You should start to see little crystals of salt on the surface. Soon, you won't need the magnifying glass at all, because the entire surface of the soil will be covered with these crystals. It will be really crusty, too. If you were trying to grow crops, would this soil work?

Supplies

- shallow dish
- salt
- soil
- water
- magnifying glass

GLOSSARY

ancestor: people from your family or country that lived before you.

additive: something added to food to change its characteristics.

aeroponics: a system of growing plants without any medium for their roots at all.

agriculture: production of food through farming.

allergen: something that triggers an allergic reaction.

amino acids: chemicals that make up protein.

antioxidant: a substance in food that helps fight disease.

bacteria: microorganisms found in soil, water, plants, and animals that are sometimes harmful.

biodegradable: something that living organisms can break down.

bioplastics: plastic made from plant material.

carbohydrates: one of the basic building blocks of nutrition, that give you energy.

carnivore: an animal that eats other animals.

climate: average weather patterns in an area over a period of many years.

commercial: large businesses producing large quantities.

complex carbohydrate: a food source such as whole grains or beans that gives you steady energy.

culture: the beliefs and customs of a group of people.

dehydrate: to remove the moisture from something.

dehydration: dangerous loss of body fluids.

digestive tract: the passage between the mouth and the anus, including the stomach and other organs that food passes through for digestion and elimination as waste.

drought: a period of very dry weather when there is not enough rain.

durable: able to last.

edible: safe to eat.

embalm: to preserve a body.

environment: a natural area with plants and animals.

environmentalist: someone who works to preserve the environment.

enzyme: a natural chemical that causes a reaction.

essential fatty acids: necessary substances found in fish and some plants that your body can't make on its own.

ethical: acting in a way that upholds someone's belief in right and wrong.

ethylene gas: a natural ripening agent produced by many fruits and vegetables.

evaporate: change from a liquid to a gas.

expiration date: the date food should be eaten by.

famine: a period of great hunger and lack of food for a large population of people.

fermentation: a chemical reaction that breaks down food.

fertile: land that's able to produce vegetation.

fertilizers: something added to soil to make it more fertile.

flood: when a dry area is covered by water.

fortified: when certain foods have nutrients added to it.

free-range: animals who are allowed to graze in open areas instead of being confined to an enclosure.

genetic engineering: manipulating genes to alter appearance and other characteristics.

glucose: a basic sugar that provides energy.

gravitropism: the ability of plants to detect and grow roots in the direction of gravity.

greenhouse effect: when gases in the atmosphere permit sunlight to pass through but then trap heat, causing the warming of the earth's surface.

greenhouse gases: carbon monoxide and other gases that get into the atmosphere and trap heat.

heirloom plants: plants that were grown earlier in human history.

herbicides: chemicals used to kill unwanted plants like weeds.

herbivore: an animal that eats only plants.

histamines: chemicals that protect the body against allergens.

hormones: compounds that work with specific organs in your body.

humanely: treating a living creature with compassion.

hydroponics: growing plants without soil.

immigrant: someone settling in a new country.

Industrial Revolution: the name of the period of time that started in the late 1700s in England when machines replaced people as a way of manufacturing.

innovation: new idea or invention.

irrigation: any method to water crops.

leaching: when water washes substances out of the soil.

legumes: plants with seeds that grow in pods, like peas and beans.

livestock: animals on a farm that produce food like milk and eggs, or products like wool.

locavore: someone who eats foods grown locally whenever possible.

longevity: how long food lasts.

macronutrients: protein, carbohydrates, and fats needed by the body in relatively large quantities every day.

malaria: a deadly, infectious disease.

micronutrients: vitamins and minerals needed by the body in small quantities every day.

microorganism: anything living that is so small you can only see it with a microscope.

migrate: to travel to the same place at the same time each year.

Nile River: a long river in Africa (4,132 miles or 6,650 kilometers) that winds its way from Burundi to Egypt.

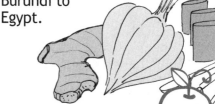

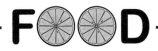

nitrogen: a naturally occurring element needed by plants.

nomads: people who move from place to place in search of food.

non-renewable: energy sources that can be used up, that we can't make more of, such as oil.

nutrients: substances that strengthen or build up your body.

nutrition: the vitamins, minerals, and other things in food that your body uses to stay healthy and grow.

omnivore: an animal that eats both plants and animals.

opaque: not clear.

organic: food grown or raised according to certain standards, without artificial fertilizers, perticides, or hormones.

organism: anything living.

osteoporosis: loss of bone density.

palatable: when something tastes okay.

pasteurized: food that has been heated to destroy harmful bacteria.

perishable: easily spoiled.

pesticides: chemicals used to kill or control insects.

pharmaceuticals: drugs used for medications.

potato blight: a disease that destroys potato crops.

preserve: to save food in a way that it won't spoil, so it can be eaten later.

prey: an animal caught or hunted for food.

produce: fruits and vegetables.

protein: one of the basic building blocks of nutrition.

rationing: when the supply of something is limited and it is distributed carefully among people.

recalled: when an entire batch of food is returned to the manufacturer because of a safety issue.

regulated: controlled by rules or laws.

salting: using salt to preserve food.

saturated fat: the fat that is the main cause of high blood cholesterol from what you eat. Butter and coconut oil have high amounts of saturated fat.

sodium: found in salt.

solder: to fuse metal together to form one piece.

sustainable: a resource that cannot be used up, such as solar energy.

typhus: a contagious disease.

vegan: a vegetarian who won't eat anything that comes from an animal, like dairy or eggs.

vegetarian: someone who eats a plant-based diet.

water cycle: the continuous movement of water from the earth to the clouds and back again.

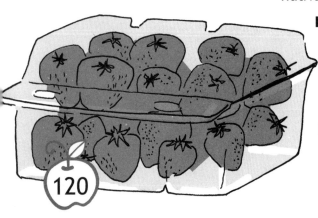

120

RESOURCES

BOOKS

Ballard, Carol. *Is Our Food Safe?* Franklin Watts, 2008.

Baines, John. *Food and Farming (The Global Village)*. Smart Apple Media, 2008.

Cobb, Vicki. *Junk Food (Where's the Science Here?)*. Millbrook Press, 2005.

Gifford, Clive. *Food and Cooking in Ancient Egypt (Cooking in World Cultures)*. PowerPress, 2010.

Jones, Charlotte. *Eat Your Words: A Fascinating Look at the Language of Food*. Delacorte Books for Young Readers, 2000.

Matthews, Rupert. *Cooking a Meal (Everyday History)*. Franklin Watts, 2000.

McCarthy, Meghan. *Pop!: The Invention of Bubble Gum*. Simon & Schuster, 2010.

Pollan, Michael. *The Omnivore's Dilemma for Kids: The Secrets Behind What You Eat*. Dial, 2009.

Solheim, James. *It's Disgusting and We Ate It! True Food Facts from Around the World and Throughout History*. Aladdin, 2001.

Taylor-Butler, Christine, *Food Safety (True Books)*. Children's Press, 2008.

WEBSITES

www.dole.com
Dole SuperKids
Games and information about nutrition and balanced diet.

www.foodtimeline.org/
Food Timeline
Basic site with long list of foods and recipes throughout history.

www.keepourfoodsafe.org/
Keep Our Food Safe
Discussion of food safety

www.molliekatzen.com/kids.php
Mollie Katzen
Kids' recipes from best-selling cooking expert, Mollie Katzen.

www.nutritionexplorations.org/ kids/main.asp
Nutrition Explorations
Explore the world of nutrition with nutrition experts.

www.pickyourown.org
Pick Your Own
Directory to find farms to pick fresh produce right near you.

www.vrg.org/family/kidsindex.htm
Vegetarian Resource Group
Information on becoming a vegetarian.

INDEX

Index